Part 1
SEASHORE LIFE

This section of the book tells you where to look for common animals, birds, fishes and plants on European coasts. It shows you lots of clues to look for, how animals and plants live in different kinds of places, and how to take notes and make collections.

Even if a beach looks deserted, you can still find out a lot about the animals that live there, by searching for tracks and other signs, such as lugworm casts.

If you want to identify something you have found, first look on the pages that deal with that kind of animal or plant. If you cannot see it there, then turn to the charts at the end of this section, where there are more species (kinds of animals or plants) to spot.

As with other hobbies, like birdwatching, a beachcomber needs some special equipment, and this is described over the page.

If you study seashore life, always be careful not to disturb animals, or pull up plants. Put shells back where you found them, and if you move rocks or stones to look under them, place them back in the same position.

In this way you will not only prevent any undue disturbance to the animals that live in the area, but you will also be able to go back to the same place and examine the same rocks for wildlife again.

Periwinkles

Common Mussel

Pod Razor Shell

Pelican's Foot Shell

Queen Scallop

Hidden Life on the Beach...

This man may think he is alone on the beach, but in fact there are living creatures all around him. They have chosen places where they are difficult to spot, and where they are least likely to be disturbed by men or other animals. The numbers show you where six of them are hidden.

Sand-Eels often bury themselves in wet sand when the tide goes out. Look for them near the surf line. They will come to the surface if the sand near them is disturbed.

Starfish usually live in the sea. If they get stranded on shore, they take shelter in pools of sea water among rocks. This one is opening a Scallop to eat it.

Gulls always nest in places that are difficult for animals to get to. They usually choose ledges on cliffs. Watch out for birds flying to or from the nests.

...and How to Find it

Goose Barnacles

Goose Barnacles grow on stalks that look like the necks of geese. These were washed ashore on driftwood. They gather food with their fringe of tentacles.

Shore Crab

This Shore Crab is hiding in a clump of seaweed in a rock pool. Use a net to hunt for crabs, and put them back in sea water when you have finished with them.

What to Take

Fishing net

Magnifying glass

Trowel

Penknife

Notebook and pencil

Spade

Plastic screw-top containers

Bucket

Sieve

You will stand a better chance of finding the things that live on the beach if you take the right equipment with you. Whenever you make a discovery, note down the time and what part of the beach you were on. Wear what you want, but put on shoes or boots for wading in rock pools, so that you don't cut your feet.

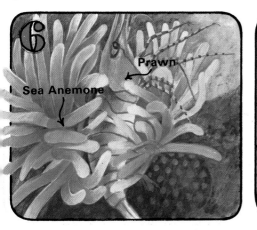
Sea Anemone — **Prawn**

Sea Anemones are flesh-eating animals that look like plants. They live on small fish and shellfish, like this prawn. Their tentacles can sting.

Barnacles under a rock

Periwinkles on seaweed

Lugworm casts on sand

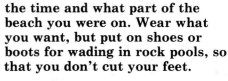
Hermit Crab in Whelk shell

The best time for exploring the beach is when the tide is furthest out. Check the local newspaper for the times of tides. Look on rocks for Barnacles and Limpets; in seaweed for Periwinkles and shellfish; under marks on wet sand for burrowing animals; and in empty shells for Hermit Crabs.

Exploring the Seashore

The kinds of animals and plants you find on the seashore will depend very much on the kind of beach you are exploring. Rocky, sandy and muddy beaches are good places to look. Shingle, or pebble, beaches are usually rather bare because the pebbles keep shifting, and at low tide they are too dry to support life. If you visit different kinds of beaches close together, notice how the creatures you find change from one beach to another. See which has more seaweeds, or more shells, where you find birds feeding, and so on.

Tides and Zones

The sea creeps up the shore, and then down again, roughly twice every 24 hours. These movements of the sea are called tides. The tides in the Mediterranean Sea are very small, and hard to notice, while the tides in other seas, like the Atlantic, are more obvious.

The highest point on the shore reached by the water is called "high water", and the lowest is called "low water". Spring tides (nothing to do with the season) happen roughly once a fortnight. They rise higher and fall lower than neap tides, which occur in between each spring tide.

The seashore can be divided into zones between the different high and low water levels. The picture below shows you the common seaweeds and shells that live in each zone.

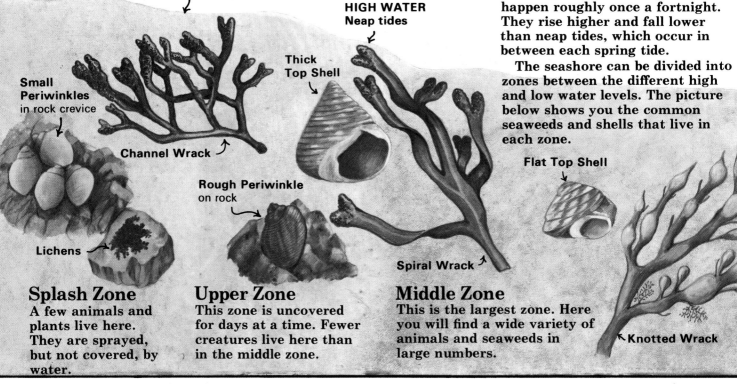

HIGH WATER Spring tides

HIGH WATER Neap tides

Thick Top Shell

Small Periwinkles in rock crevice

Channel Wrack

Rough Periwinkle on rock

Lichens

Spiral Wrack

Flat Top Shell

Knotted Wrack

Splash Zone
A few animals and plants live here. They are sprayed, but not covered, by water.

Upper Zone
This zone is uncovered for days at a time. Fewer creatures live here than in the middle zone.

Middle Zone
This is the largest zone. Here you will find a wide variety of animals and seaweeds in large numbers.

1 Types of Coastline— Rocky Shores

Purple Sandpiper

Ravens

Groynes

The movement of the sea changes the shape of rocky shores. The water wears cliffs away and pulls pieces of rock down the shore, leaving the heaviest at the top. Groynes stop the rocks being swept too far *along* the shore.

2 Sand Dunes

Ringed Plover

WIND

Grasses are often planted on dunes to help stop the sand being blown further inland. If you would like to help with planting, contact the Nature Conservancy Council.

The Mediterranean Coast

Mediterranean Gulls

Blue Rock Thrush

You can sometimes see the tide mark on rocks in the Mediterranean.

60 cm.

The seashore on the Mediterranean Sea has all the zones shown on this page, but they are telescoped into a very narrow band. The tide in the Mediterranean never rises and falls more than about 60 cm., so it is difficult to see the different zones. You will still be able, however, to find many of the plants and animals shown in this book. Look, too, for animals that can live more or less out of water, such as Land Crabs.

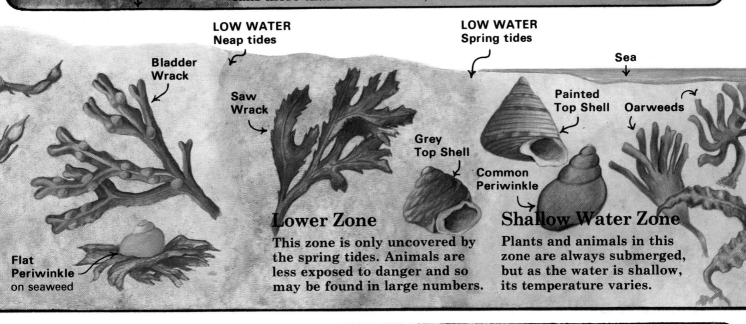

LOW WATER
Neap tides

LOW WATER
Spring tides

Sea

Bladder Wrack

Saw Wrack

Painted Top Shell

Oarweeds

Grey Top Shell

Common Periwinkle

Flat Periwinkle on seaweed

Lower Zone

This zone is only uncovered by the spring tides. Animals are less exposed to danger and so may be found in large numbers.

Shallow Water Zone

Plants and animals in this zone are always submerged, but as the water is shallow, its temperature varies.

3 Dykes

Brent Geese

Very flat coasts may be flooded by the sea. Dykes are built to hold back the water. A lot of wildlife may be found on these sheltered coasts.

Make your own Map of the Beach

String

WOOTTON BAY

2ND MAY 1976 LOW TIDE

Brown seaweed + Periwinkles

3 m. Splash Zone

7 m. Upper Zone

Thick Top Shell →

15 m. Middle Zone

Knotted Wrack

10 m. Lower Zone

Grey Top Shell →

Stretch a piece of string, tied to rocks at both ends, down the beach, and mark on your map everything that you see near the line. See if you can work out, from the seaweeds and shells you find, where the different zones begin and end. Make your map at low tide.

Seaweeds and their Secrets

You can find many kinds of seaweed growing on the shore, especially on rocky shores, and large deep-water seaweeds are often washed up after a storm. Compare them with land plants to see how well they are suited to life in the sea. Instead of growing roots, they anchor themselves to rocks or stones against the action of the waves. They take in food from the water, not the ground. Some can live both in and out of water as the tide goes in and out.

Check: some seaweeds have a thick vein, or **midrib**, running up the frond.

Check: what colour are the leaf-like branches (called **fronds**)? Are they flat or wavy, or broken along the edges?

Check: how long is the stalk, or **stipe**?

Holdfast. Check: is it disk-shaped or branched?

Brown Seaweed
Bladder wrack is one of the most common brown seaweeds. Use the check points in the picture to help you identify other seaweeds.

Some seaweeds have **air bladders**. They help to keep the plant upright in the water. Check: are they growing singly or in pairs?

Check: do fronds divide, or **branch**, or do they grow straight up from the holdfast? You can work out roughly how old Bladder Wrack is by counting two branchings for each year.

Bladder Wrack

1 At low tide seaweed growing on the shore lies flat.

2 At high tide the water holds it up.

Red Seaweed

Most red seaweeds are smaller than brown seaweeds. Look for them on rocks and in deep rock pools on the lower zone. Some feel hard and brittle, and look like coral.

Green Seaweed

Most green seaweeds are small, but they often grow in large clumps and cover rocks like a carpet. Look for them under large brown seaweeds on the upper and middle zones.

How Many Frond Shapes Can You Find?

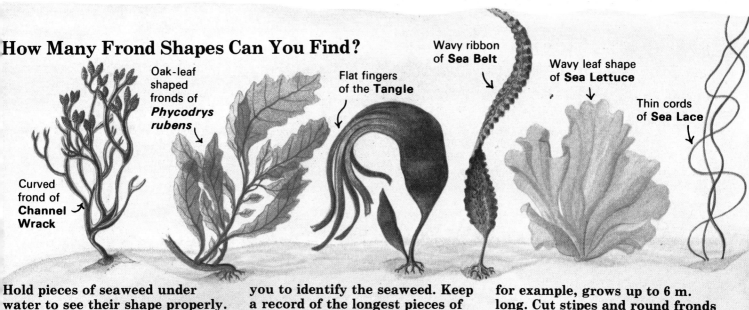

Curved frond of **Channel Wrack**

Oak-leaf shaped fronds of **Phycodrys rubens**

Flat fingers of the **Tangle**

Wavy ribbon of **Sea Belt**

Wavy leaf shape of **Sea Lettuce**

Thin cords of **Sea Lace**

Hold pieces of seaweed under water to see their shape properly. The shape of the frond will help you to identify the seaweed. Keep a record of the longest pieces of each kind that you find. Sea Lace, for example, grows up to 6 m. long. Cut stipes and round fronds in half to see if they are hollow.

Holdfasts

Most holdfasts are branched or disk-shaped. They fix the seaweeds onto the rocks. Try pulling one off its rock to see how strongly it is anchored.

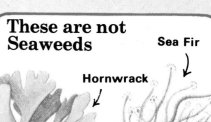

Disk

Branched

Button-shaped

These are not Seaweeds

Sea Fir

Hornwrack

These "plants" are really groups of tiny animals. Look for Sea Firs on rocks, in pools and on large seaweeds. The Hornwrack is often washed up.

Things that Grow on Seaweed

Worm galls

Look for small seaweeds and worm galls on large seaweeds.

Tufts of red seaweed on **Knotted Wrack**

Worm tubes on **Saw Wrack**

Tiny worms live in these tubes. Check which way the tube coils.

Look among seaweeds for sponges. Some squirt water if you press them.

Encrusting Sponge

Purse Sponge

Breadcrumb Sponge

HERE IS A SIMPLE – BUT NOT VERY RELIABLE – WAY OF FORECASTING THE WEATHER. FIND A PIECE OF SEA BELT. IF IT FEELS LIMP AND MOIST IT WILL RAIN. IF IT IS HARD AND DRY IT WILL BE FINE

Rock Pools

A beach with rock pools can be one of the most exciting to explore. Here you will find animals that cannot survive out of water when the tide is out, as well as animals and plants that also live elsewhere on the shore. Look especially in pools with seaweed, which protects the animals from the sun and keeps the water temperature more even. Wear shoes that will not slip on wet rocks.

On windy days, when the surface of the rock pool is disturbed, look through the bottom of a clear plastic box to see into the pool. Keep very still and wait for animals to come out of hiding.

ALWAYS put rocks back the right way up to protect the animals living underneath.

Sea Anemones

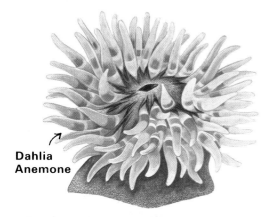

Dahlia Anemone

Sea anemones are animals. This one is usually camouflaged with bits of shell and gravel. If you prod it, it squirts water and contracts.

How a Beadlet Anemone Eats

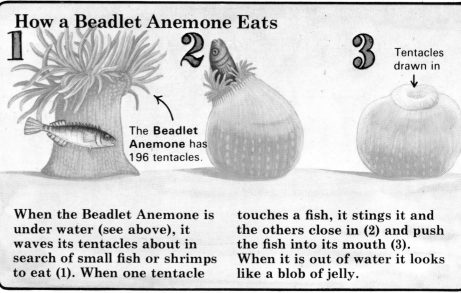

1

2

3 Tentacles drawn in

The **Beadlet Anemone** has 196 tentacles.

When the Beadlet Anemone is under water (see above), it waves its tentacles about in search of small fish or shrimps to eat (1). When one tentacle touches a fish, it stings it and the others close in (2) and push the fish into its mouth (3). When it is out of water it looks like a blob of jelly.

Shore Crab

The Shore Crab is common on the middle and lower zones. A crab carries its tail under its body. Check how many joints it has. Some also hide their fourth pair of legs.

Spider Crab

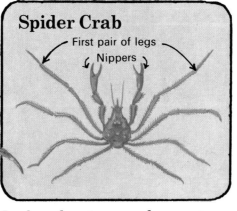

First pair of legs
Nippers

Look under stones and among seaweed on the lower zone for this crab. Its shell is about 1 cm. across. Notice the length of the first pair of legs.

Sea Urchin

The Sea Urchin's spines drop off when it dies. Some live on rocks and have a strong round shell. Other types burrow in the sand and have a more delicate, oval shell.

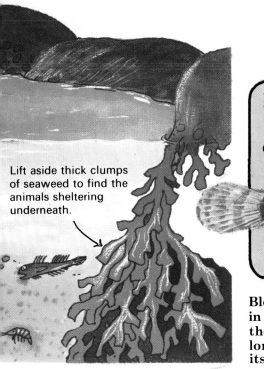

Lift aside thick clumps of seaweed to find the animals sheltering underneath.

Fish

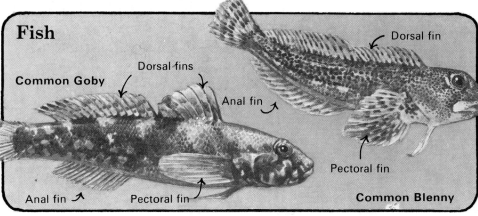

Common Goby

Dorsal fins

Anal fin

Anal fin

Pectoral fin

Dorsal fin

Pectoral fin

Common Blenny

Blennies and Gobies are common in pools. Look at the fins to tell them apart. The Blenny has one long dorsal fin (the Goby has two), its anal fin is nearer the tail than the Goby's, and it has spiky pectoral fins (the Goby's are smoother and longer.)

Shrimps and Prawns

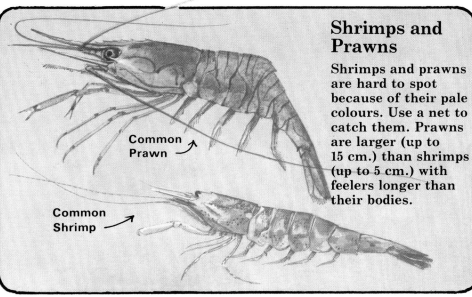

Common Prawn

Common Shrimp

Shrimps and prawns are hard to spot because of their pale colours. Use a net to catch them. Prawns are larger (up to 15 cm.) than shrimps (up to 5 cm.) with feelers longer than their bodies.

Brittle Stars

Look in pools among Coralline seaweeds for Brittle Stars. Handle them gently as their long thin arms break off easily.

Sea Hare

Starfish

Common Starfish

Common Sunstar

Cushion Star

This Sea Hare has its shell in its body. It changes colour with age, from red to brown, then dark green. In summer, look for strings of its orange spawn round Oarweeds.

Most starfish have five arms, but the Common Sunstar has up to 13. Look on the lower zone.

Look through a lens to see the rows of tube-feet (suckers) which pull the starfish along. Look in shallow shaded pools for the short-armed Cushion Star.

Flowers and Grasses

Many plants that grow by the sea are also found inland, but the seashore plants have to protect themselves against the salt spray and strong winds. Look at the leaves, the roots and the shape of the plants to see the differences. Some flowers can grow on any beach—even on shingle. Make a note of where you find flowers, and see if you can find the same flower on a different kind of beach.

Hawthorn is one of the few trees that grows by the sea. The wind dries out the soil on one side of the tree, so that its roots and branches only develop on the side away from the wind. They look as though they are being swept away.

Dunes

The picture shows how plants help to form dunes. The grasses have very long roots which hold down the sand in ridges, and stop the wind blowing the sand away. Marram grass is the most common.

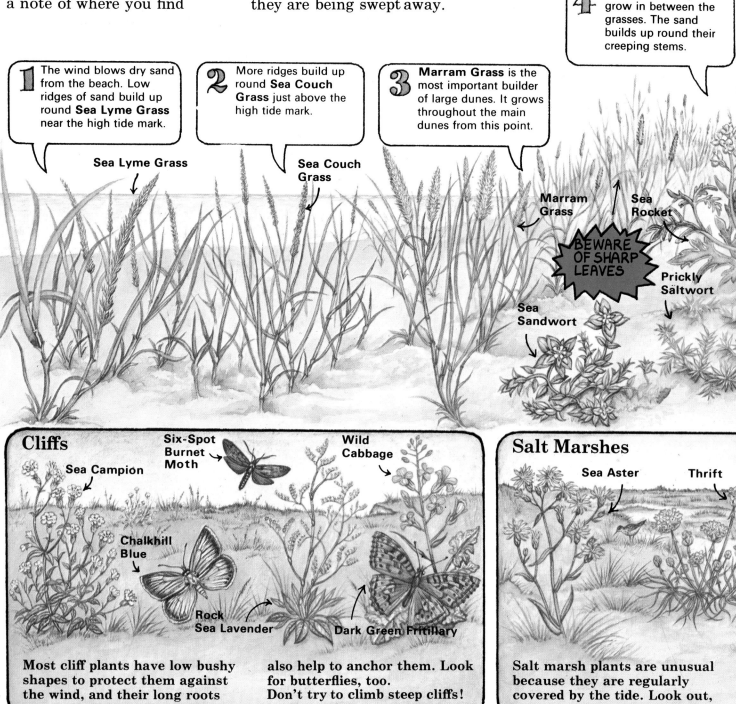

4 Small plants begin to grow in between the grasses. The sand builds up round their creeping stems.

1 The wind blows dry sand from the beach. Low ridges of sand build up round **Sea Lyme Grass** near the high tide mark.

2 More ridges build up round **Sea Couch Grass** just above the high tide mark.

3 **Marram Grass** is the most important builder of large dunes. It grows throughout the main dunes from this point.

Sea Lyme Grass

Sea Couch Grass

Marram Grass

Sea Rocket

BEWARE OF SHARP LEAVES

Sea Sandwort

Prickly Saltwort

Cliffs

Sea Campion

Six-Spot Burnet Moth

Wild Cabbage

Chalkhill Blue

Rock Sea Lavender

Dark Green Fritillary

Most cliff plants have low bushy shapes to protect them against the wind, and their long roots also help to anchor them. Look for butterflies, too.
Don't try to climb steep cliffs!

Salt Marshes

Sea Aster

Thrift

Salt marsh plants are unusual because they are regularly covered by the tide. Look out,

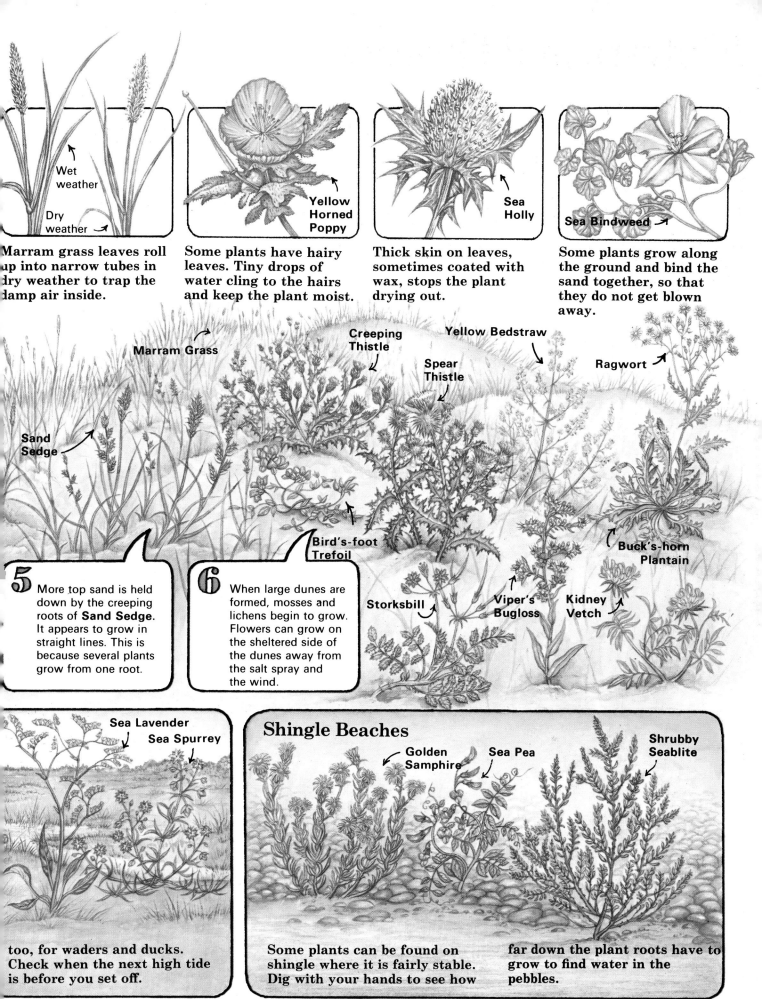

Wet weather

Dry weather

Yellow Horned Poppy

Sea Holly

Sea Bindweed

Marram grass leaves roll up into narrow tubes in dry weather to trap the damp air inside.

Some plants have hairy leaves. Tiny drops of water cling to the hairs and keep the plant moist.

Thick skin on leaves, sometimes coated with wax, stops the plant drying out.

Some plants grow along the ground and bind the sand together, so that they do not get blown away.

Marram Grass

Creeping Thistle

Yellow Bedstraw

Spear Thistle

Ragwort

Sand Sedge

Bird's-foot Trefoil

Buck's-horn Plantain

5 More top sand is held down by the creeping roots of **Sand Sedge**. It appears to grow in straight lines. This is because several plants grow from one root.

6 When large dunes are formed, mosses and lichens begin to grow. Flowers can grow on the sheltered side of the dunes away from the salt spray and the wind.

Storksbill

Viper's Bugloss

Kidney Vetch

Sea Lavender

Sea Spurrey

Shingle Beaches

Golden Samphire

Sea Pea

Shrubby Seablite

too, for waders and ducks. Check when the next high tide is before you set off.

Some plants can be found on shingle where it is fairly stable. Dig with your hands to see how

far down the plant roots have to grow to find water in the pebbles.

Collecting Shells

The empty shells you find on the beach once belonged to molluscs—soft-bodied animals without internal skeletons. Some molluscs live on the shore. Others live in the sea, but you may find their shells washed up on the shore. To identify your shell, you must first decide which group of molluscs it belongs to. Some will be gastropods, which have a single, usually coiled shell, like Whelks and Periwinkles.

Check whether your gastropod shell coils clockwise or anti-clockwise as you look down on its pointed top.

Bivalves are molluscs with two (bi) shells (or valves), held together by muscles. Empty bivalve shells often break apart in the sea, but if you find both halves together, see if they are the same shape and size, as in Mussels, or unequal, as in Scallops.

Shapes and Colours

Shell colours show up best when the shells are wet. Some shells vary in colour. You could make a collection of shells of the same kind with different colours. The shape of shells can vary, too, depending on where they live.

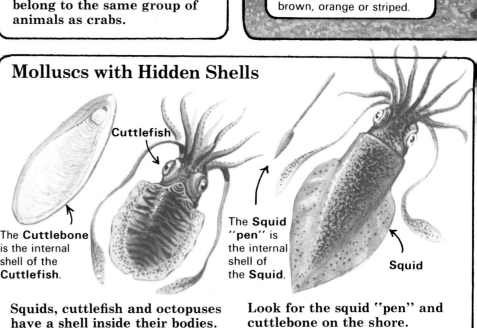

Look for **Flat Periwinkles** on Bladder or Knotted Wrack. They can be yellow, brown, orange or striped.

Gastropods

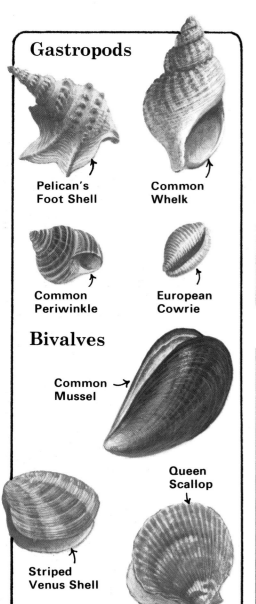

Pelican's Foot Shell

Common Whelk

Common Periwinkle

European Cowrie

Bivalves

Common Mussel

Queen Scallop

Striped Venus Shell

These are not Molluscs

Acorn Barnacles

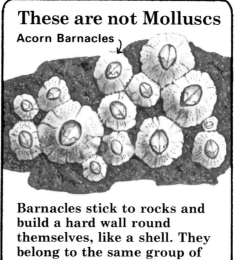

Barnacles stick to rocks and build a hard wall round themselves, like a shell. They belong to the same group of animals as crabs.

Molluscs with Hidden Shells

Cuttlefish

The **Cuttlebone** is the internal shell of the **Cuttlefish**.

The **Squid** "pen" is the internal shell of the **Squid**.

Squid

Squids, cuttlefish and octopuses have a shell inside their bodies.

Look for the squid "pen" and cuttlebone on the shore.

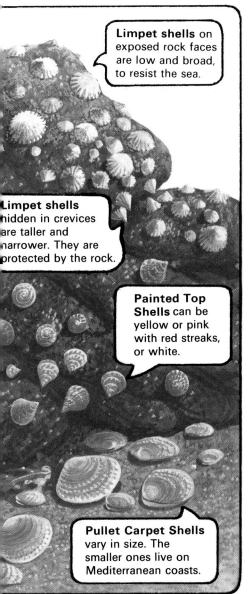

Limpet shells on exposed rock faces are low and broad, to resist the sea.

Limpet shells hidden in crevices are taller and narrower. They are protected by the rock.

Painted Top Shells can be yellow or pink with red streaks, or white.

Pullet Carpet Shells vary in size. The smaller ones live on Mediterranean coasts.

Shells with Holes

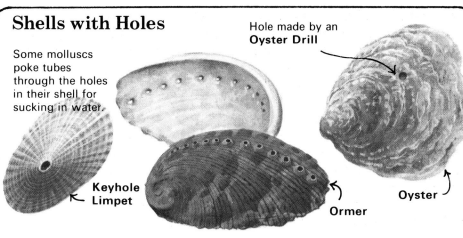

Some molluscs poke tubes through the holes in their shell for sucking in water.

Hole made by an **Oyster Drill**

Keyhole Limpet

Ormer

Oyster

Holes in shells are either used for sucking in water, or are made by molluscs that drill holes in the shells of other molluscs. The Oyster Drill feeds on Oysters in this way.

1 How to Collect Shells

Thick paper for labels

Magnifying glass

Pen

Plastic bags

Bucket

Trowel

Take these things with you. Search low down on the shore, on rocks, under seaweed and stones, in pools and in the sand.

2

Label

Put each shell in a separate bag, with a label saying where you found it.

3

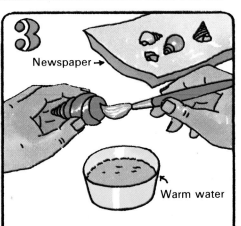

Newspaper →

Warm water

When you get home, clean your shells in warm water with a soft brush. Leave them to dry on newspaper.

4

Shoe box

Varnish

Cotton wool

Sticky label

Brush a thin coat of varnish on each shell. Keep your collection *either* in a shoe box lined with cotton wool . . .

5

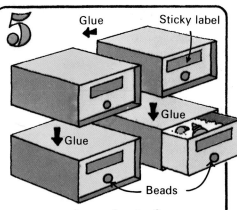

Glue

Sticky label

Glue

Glue

Beads

. . . *or* make a chest of drawers by sticking together several large matchboxes. Label the fronts and sew on beads for handles.

Looking at Shells

This picture shows where molluscs live, how they feed, how they fix themselves to rocks so they are not washed away by the sea, and how some can live both in and out of the water. Some gastropods eat seaweed. They file off bits of the plant with their rough "tongue". Others use the "tongue" to drill a hole in the shells of other molluscs, and scrape off bits of the animal inside. Most bivalves suck in sea water and feed off the tiny plants and animals in it.

Follow the Limpet

Mark some Limpets and the rock next to them with quick-drying paint. When you go back in a few hours, you will be able to see how far they have moved.

Limpets feed on seaweed spores. They fix themselves to the rock with a very strong foot. Try pulling one off to see how strong it is.

Slipper Limpets grow on top of one another in chains of up to nine.

Saddle Oyster shells follow the shape of the rock so that they cannot be washed away.

Look for **Blue-rayed Limpets** on Oarweeds, which they feed on. The young Limpets have bright blue rays across the shell.

The **Common Wentletrap** is a very beautiful tall, thin shell found very low down on the shore.

Rarer Shells
These shells are rather less common than the ones in the main picture.

Chinaman's Hat

Tower Shell

Smooth Venus

Heart Cockle

Beer Barrel Shell

Pheasant Shell

Watching Cliff Birds

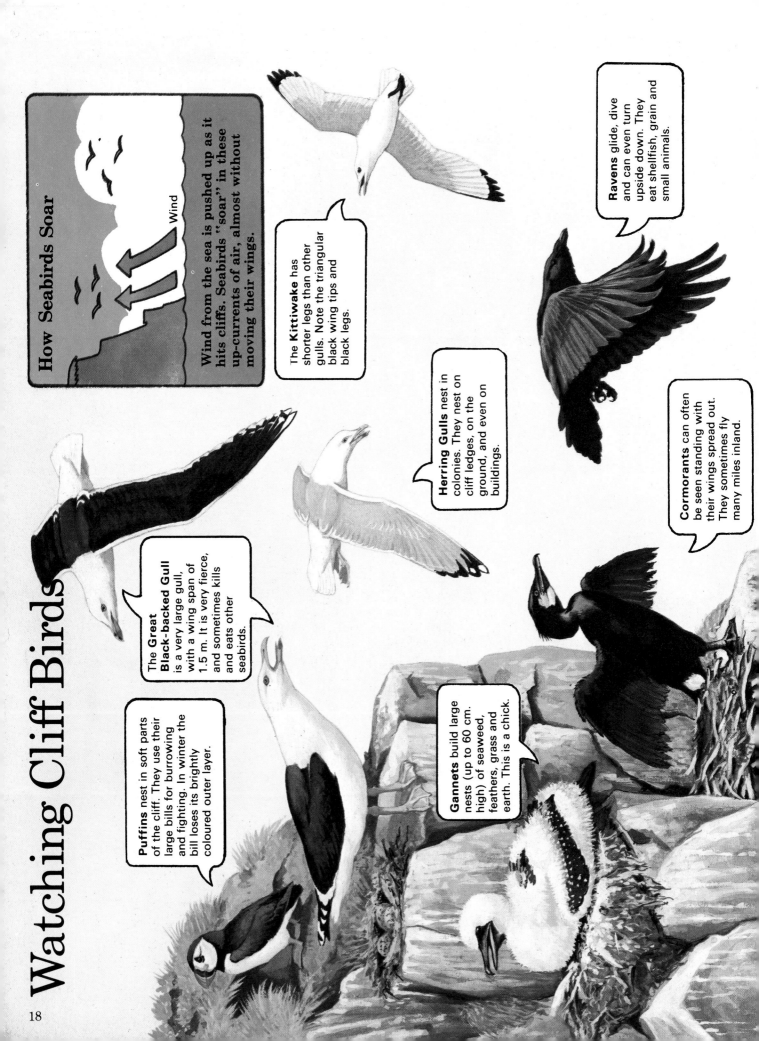

How Seabirds Soar

Wind

Wind from the sea is pushed up as it hits cliffs. Seabirds "soar" in these up-currents of air, almost without moving their wings.

The **Kittiwake** has shorter legs than other gulls. Note the triangular black wing tips and black legs.

Ravens glide, dive and can even turn upside down. They eat shellfish, grain and small animals.

Herring Gulls nest in colonies. They nest on cliff ledges, on the ground, and even on buildings.

Cormorants can often be seen standing with their wings spread out. They sometimes fly many miles inland.

The **Great Black-backed Gull** is a very large gull, with a wing span of 1.5 m. It is very fierce, and sometimes kills and eats other seabirds.

Puffins nest in soft parts of the cliff. They use their large bills for burrowing and fighting. In winter the bill loses its brightly coloured outer layer.

Gannets build large nests (up to 60 cm. high) of seaweed, feathers, grass and earth. This is a chick.

The **Razorbill** has a stout body with short wings. It flies fast and swims well.

Manx Shearwaters almost touch the water as they glide over the sea. They are easy to recognize as they are black on top, white underneath.

The **Storm Petrel**, our smallest seabird, flutters over the water looking for plankton and small fish. Note the square-shaped tail.

Guillemots dive from the surface to catch fish. They can stay under water for up to a minute.

The **Fulmar** is fatter and fluffier than gulls. It glides on stiff wings, using the wind currents along the cliff face.

Gannets dive 30 m. or more to catch fish, which they swallow whole. Note the black wing tips, snowy white plumage, and strong flight with regular wing beats.

The **Shag** is very like the Cormorant, but it is smaller and thinner. It has a fast, direct flight, and often perches on rocks.

The **Kittiwake**, a small gull, makes a nest of green seaweed stuck to the cliff with mud.

Razorbills nest in colonies, laying their single egg in a crevice or under a boulder on the cliff.

Guillemots lay a single egg on bare rock. The egg is pear-shaped, so it rolls round instead of falling off the cliff.

REMEMBER! DON'T GO NEAR THE CLIFF EDGE OR TRY TO CLIMB CLIFFS. NEVER TAKE BIRDS' EGGS OR DISTURB THEIR NESTING PLACES.

All these birds nest on cliffs or rocky islands. Some nest in groups, called colonies, which you may be able to visit. But even if you cannot get very close to the birds, it is still interesting to watch them in flight, and possible to identify many of them.

19

Birds on the Beach

Salt marshes and muddy shores are good places to look for waders, ducks and geese. Look for waders, gulls, and terns on sandy beaches. Some of these birds migrate from the far north in winter to find better feeding places. Notice especially how the birds you see move on the ground, and how they feed, to help you to identify them. Remember that many birds change their plumage in winter, often becoming duller in colour.

1 Keeping Safe

Little Tern's egg

Birds that nest on the shore have eggs that are patterned to blend in with the sand or stones where they are laid.

2

Redshank on nest

Some birds build nests that blend in with the background to hide them from enemies. The Redshank builds its nest with grass in a tuft of grass.

The **Herring Gull** drops shells from the air onto rocks to burst them open.

The **Sanderling** darts along the tide line looking for shrimps, molluscs and worms.

Black-headed Gulls paddle in wet sand to bring animals to the surface.

The **Common Tern** dives to catch small fish, especially Sand-Eels.

The **Redshank** probes in the sand for worms and small molluscs.

A baby **Herring Gull** will beg for food by pecking at a red spot on the parent's bill.

Turnstones use their short sharp bills to find animals under stones and seaweed.

The male **Little Tern**, like other terns, gives Sand-Eels to the female in the courtship ceremony.

The **Bar-tailed Godwit** probes wet mud for insects and molluscs to eat.

The **Oystercatcher** uses its bill to dislodge Limpets and prise open Mussels to eat.

3 **Ringed Plover** dragging its wing

Some birds pretend to be hurt if their eggs or chicks are in danger. The enemy then follows the parent bird, instead of attacking the nest.

Danger from Oil

Cormorant

When birds get covered in oil emptied into the sea from tankers, they cannot fly or swim, and many starve to death or swallow the oil when preening, and poison themselves. The oil mats the bird's feathers together. Then the bird can no longer keep a layer of warm air under its feathers, so many die of cold.

Sometimes, however, they can be saved. If you find a live bird coated in oil, contact the local RSPCA clinic. Do not try to clean the bird yourself.

1 **Identifying Birds**

Oystercatcher

Manx Shearwater has long straight wings

Lapwing has broad, rounded wings

What shape are the bird's wings? Look to see if they are long or short, pointed or rounded, if the feathers are separated at the wing tips.

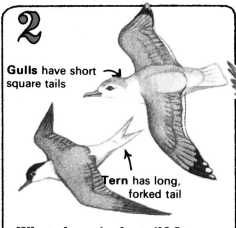

2

Gulls have short square tails

Tern has long, forked tail

What shape is the tail? It might be long or short, square or rounded, forked or cleft.

3 **Guillemot** flies straight and fast

Fulmar glides on stiff wings

How does it fly? In a straight or wavy line? Does it glide? If it is a diving bird, does it dive from the air or from the water's surface?

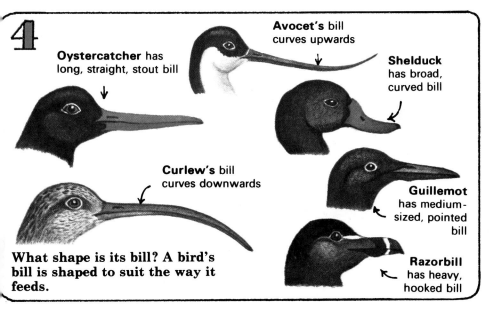

4

Oystercatcher has long, straight, stout bill

Avocet's bill curves upwards

Shelduck has broad, curved bill

Curlew's bill curves downwards

Guillemot has medium-sized, pointed bill

Razorbill has heavy, hooked bill

What shape is its bill? A bird's bill is shaped to suit the way it feeds.

5

Grey Plover has black patches under wings in winter

Dunlin has black belly

Kittiwake has black wing-tips and legs

Has it any special marks? Look on top and underneath for patches or stripes of colour. What colours are the bill and legs?

Animal Life in the Sand and Mud

At first sight a sandy beach may look empty. But if you dig down you can find many animals that burrow, especially on sheltered beaches where the sand is stable. There are no clear zones in the sand, because the conditions stay the same in spite of the tides. The animals simply burrow deeper to find moisture when the tide is out. You will find more animals near the surface if you dig along the low tide mark.

Animals that Live in Mud

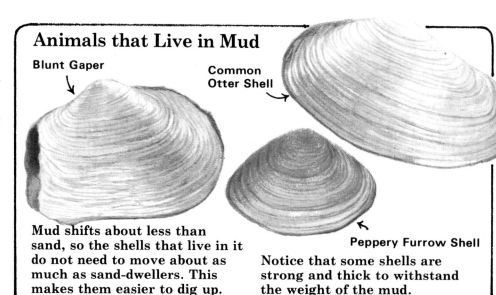

Blunt Gaper

Common Otter Shell

Peppery Furrow Shell

Mud shifts about less than sand, so the shells that live in it do not need to move about as much as sand-dwellers. This makes them easier to dig up.

Notice that some shells are strong and thick to withstand the weight of the mud.

The **Sand Mason** worm builds a tube of sand and bits of shell around itself.

Signs on the Sand

Look out for clues on the surface of the sand that give away the hiding places of burrowing animals. You will have to dig down fast to catch up with them.

Empty **Actaeon** shells mean live ones are probably buried in the sand beneath.

Lugworm hollows and casts show where the two ends of the worm's burrow are.

Most **bivalves** live in the sand. You may see them disappearing as you approach. They often live in large groups. Some have ribbed shells to anchor them in the sand.

The **Netted Whelk** is one of the few gastropods that lives in the sand. Look out for its feeding siphon sticking up as it ploughs along the surface. Note the ribs on its shell that give it its name.

The **Sea Potato** is a heart urchin. Look out for the dent it leaves above its burrow.

Lugworm in U-shaped burrow

The **Masked Crab** lives in sand in the lower zone. It has a mask-like pattern on its shell.

The **Lesser Sand-Eel** is a common shore fish. Find it buried in sand in bays during spring and summer.

The **Sea Cucumber** is an animal, not a plant. This one can grow up to 30 cm. long.

Lesser Weever Fish ↗

DON'T TOUCH! WATCH OUT FOR THIS FISH ON OR IN SAND, ESPECIALLY WHERE THERE ARE A LOT OF SHRIMPS, ON WHICH IT FEEDS. THE SPINES ON ITS FINS ARE POISONOUS

A Burrowing Starfish

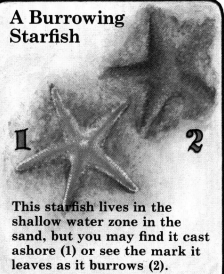

This starfish lives in the shallow water zone in the sand, but you may find it cast ashore (1) or see the mark it leaves as it burrows (2).

Look Under Heart Urchins

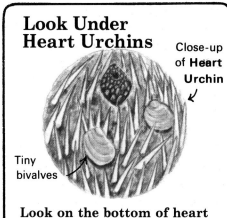

Close-up of **Heart Urchin** ↙

Tiny bivalves ↗

Look on the bottom of heart urchins among the spines for tiny bivalves that live there. Handle urchins gently as their spines rub off easily.

How Razor Shells Burrow

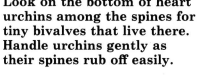

A Razor Shell has a "foot" which it pushes out of one end of its shell. It can dig very fast by contracting and expanding this foot. First it pulls itself upright (1, 2) then pushes the foot into the sand and pulls itself down (3, 4).

Worms in the Sand

Bootlace Worm ↙

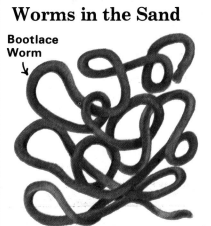

The Bootlace Worm is usually 5 m. long. It lies in coils under stones on muddy shingle.

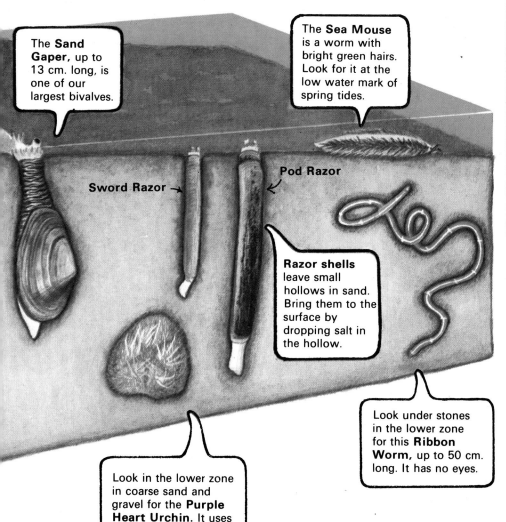

The **Sand Gaper,** up to 13 cm. long, is one of our largest bivalves.

The **Sea Mouse** is a worm with bright green hairs. Look for it at the low water mark of spring tides.

Sword Razor →

Pod Razor ↙

Razor shells leave small hollows in sand. Bring them to the surface by dropping salt in the hollow.

Look in the lower zone in coarse sand and gravel for the **Purple Heart Urchin**. It uses its spines to burrow.

Look under stones in the lower zone for this **Ribbon Worm**, up to 50 cm. long. It has no eyes.

23

Fishes

Some kinds of fish are more difficult to identify than others because their colours vary between the male and female, and between adults and young. Look for fish in pools, estuaries, and shallow water in bays. Remember that some, like eels, spend part of their life in the sea and part in fresh water. Some fish feed on seaweed and plankton, others on worms, molluscs and other fish.

Flat Fish

Look in the shallow water zone for these flat fish. You will only find small specimens —the larger ones live in deep water. Notice how their colours act as a camouflage. They hide by flapping their fins on the sea bottom to cover themselves with sand.

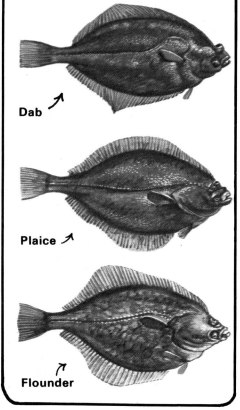

Dab

Plaice

Flounder

The **Lumpsucker** has a large, strong sucker on its underside for fixing itself to rocks. It has no scales, but notice the rows of lumps, called tubercles, on its body.

The **Spotted Goby** swims in shoals among seaweed just below low tide mark, and in harbours.

Lesser Sand-Eels swim in large shoals over sand. Their silvery colour makes them hard to see.

Look in weedy rock pools for the **15-Spined Stickleback**. In spring the male builds, guards and cleans its nest.

The **Grey Gurnard** lives on the seabed. It probes the bottom with feelers to find worms and crustaceans to eat.

Montagu's Sea Snail has a sucker, but no scales or tubercles. Look under seaweed. It lays its eggs on Oarweed holdfasts and rocks.

The **Tompot Blenny** is found low down on rocky shores. It grows to about 30 cm. long.

The **Butterfish** (or **Gunnel**) is a relative of the Blenny. It has a flat body and rounded tail, and a very slippery skin. It lives under rocks.

The **Sand** or **Common Goby** is patterned like the sand. Notice the dark spot on its dorsal fin. Gobies have a fin underneath which forms a weak sucker.

Conger Eels, up to 2 m. long, hide in cracks and under stones in the lower zone of rocky shores. They come out at night to feed. Beware of their sharp teeth!

Look in eelgrass very low down on the shore for the **Greater Pipe-Fish**. It has a long snout.

Look under seaweed in small pools for the **Long-Spined Sea Scorpion**. Its spines are sharp, but not poisonous.

The **Cornish Sucker** hides under stones. It has a strong sucker on its underside.

The **Corkwing Wrasse** hides in crevices. Wrasses are very colourful, heavily-built fish with thick lips and strong teeth.

Beachcombing

Above or on the high water level, you will see a line of dead seaweed and rubbish thrown up by the sea onto the beach. This is called the strand line. If you look more closely, you may find some interesting things, some alive, others dead. It is also a good place to look for animals and birds that find their food among this rubbish, like Sandhoppers, beetles, flies, gulls and Turnstones.

Some beachcombers hunt along the strand line for shipping objects, like cork and glass floats, old bottles, and fishing nets.

Things that Look like Stones

Belemnite

This is the fossil of an animal related to squids and octopuses.

Ammonite

Bean

This coiled fossil is the remains of an animal that lived millions of years ago. It shows the shape of the animal's shell.

This bean-shaped object is the fruit of a West Indian plant, up to 5 cm. across.

A relative of the jellyfish, the **Portuguese Man-o'-War** may be cast ashore. Do not touch! This animal can sting.

Egg cases on little stalks belong to the **Common Dog Whelk**. Look in rock crevices.

Aurelia aurita is a very common jellyfish.

Look in the lower zone on Eel Grass for rows of flat **egg cases of Netted Dog Whelks**.

Crab shell

Egg cases of Netted Dog Whelk

Crab shell

Egg case of a Ray. These, and the cases of Dogfish, are called "mermaid's purses".

Dogfish egg cases have long tendrils. They will probably be empty.

Look for **empty crab shells**. As crabs get bigger, they shed their shells and grow a skin, which hardens to form a new shell.

Dead Animals

Fish tag

Bird rings and tags

Bird ring

147 FZP
147

42013

27913

31041

Seal tag

Animals are ringed so that their movements can be traced. If you find any of these animals dead on the beach, look for a ring or tag. Send any that you find to the address on the tag, with a note of where and when you found it.

REMEMBER — NEVER EAT ANYTHING YOU FIND ON THE BEACH, DEAD OR ALIVE. WATCH OUT FOR BROKEN GLASS AND OIL. YOU CAN CLEAN OIL OFF YOUR FEET WITH EUCALYPTUS OIL AND COTTON WOOL

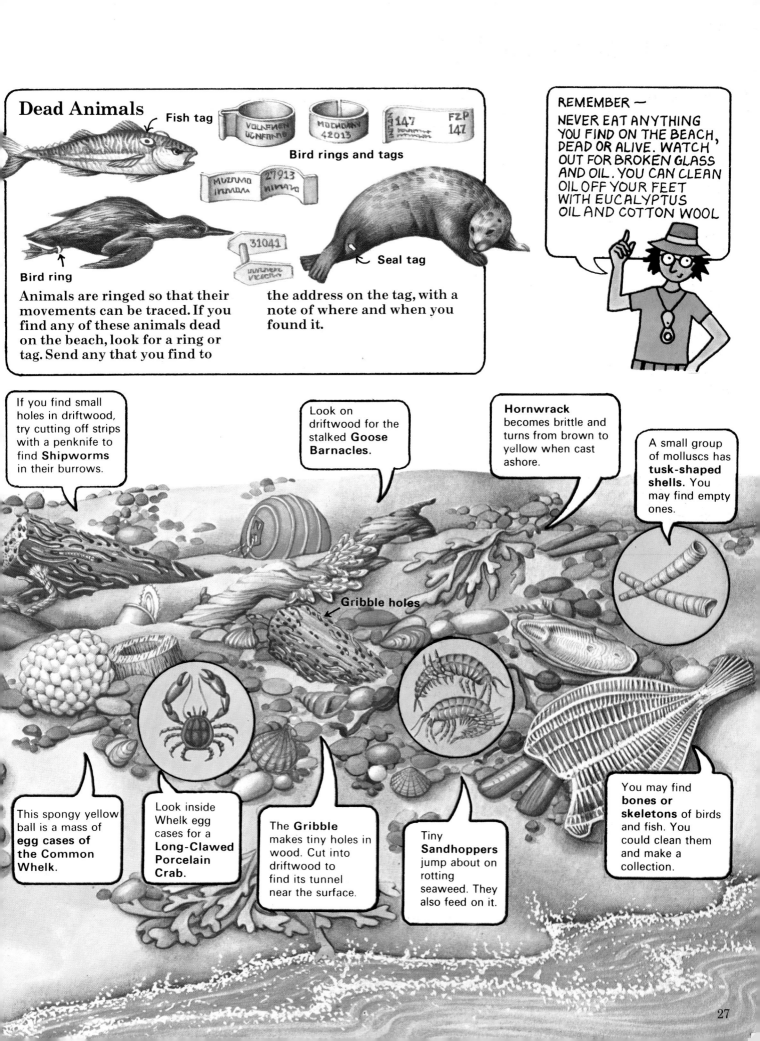

If you find small holes in driftwood, try cutting off strips with a penknife to find **Shipworms** in their burrows.

Look on driftwood for the stalked **Goose Barnacles**.

Hornwrack becomes brittle and turns from brown to yellow when cast ashore.

A small group of molluscs has **tusk-shaped shells**. You may find empty ones.

Gribble holes

This spongy yellow ball is a mass of **egg cases of the Common Whelk**.

Look inside Whelk egg cases for a **Long-Clawed Porcelain Crab**.

The **Gribble** makes tiny holes in wood. Cut into driftwood to find its tunnel near the surface.

Tiny **Sandhoppers** jump about on rotting seaweed. They also feed on it.

You may find **bones or skeletons** of birds and fish. You could clean them and make a collection.

27

More Seashore Life to Spot

Fishes

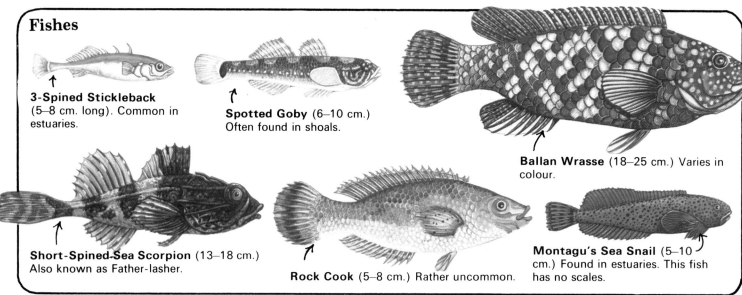

3-Spined Stickleback (5–8 cm. long). Common in estuaries.

Spotted Goby (6–10 cm.) Often found in shoals.

Ballan Wrasse (18–25 cm.) Varies in colour.

Short-Spined Sea Scorpion (13–18 cm.) Also known as Father-lasher.

Rock Cook (5–8 cm.) Rather uncommon.

Montagu's Sea Snail (5–10 cm.) Found in estuaries. This fish has no scales.

Jellyfish

Common Jellyfish (8–20 cm. across) →

Rhizostoma octopus (up to 60 cm. across)

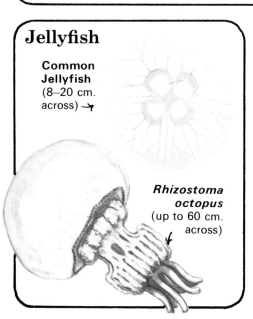

Anemones and Corals

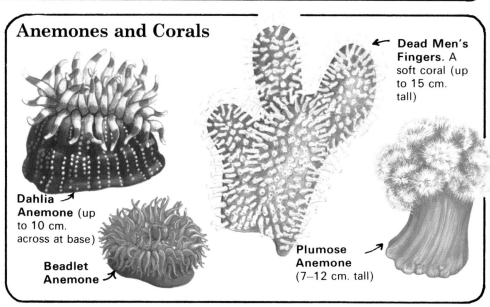

Dead Men's Fingers. A soft coral (up to 15 cm. tall)

Dahlia Anemone (up to 10 cm. across at base)

Beadlet Anemone

Plumose Anemone (7–12 cm. tall)

Sponges

Breadcrumb Sponge Grows on rocks and seaweeds.

Purse Sponge Grows under rocks, in pools, and among seaweed.

Worms

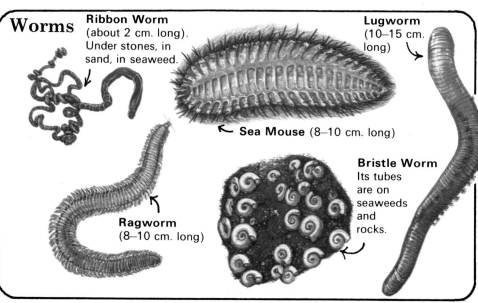

Ribbon Worm (about 2 cm. long). Under stones, in sand, in seaweed.

Lugworm (10–15 cm. long)

Sea Mouse (8–10 cm. long)

Ragworm (8–10 cm. long)

Bristle Worm Its tubes are on seaweeds and rocks.

Remember—if you cannot see a picture of the thing that you want to identify on these pages, turn to the page earlier in the book that deals with that kind of animal or plant.

Note: the animals in these boxes are not drawn to scale.

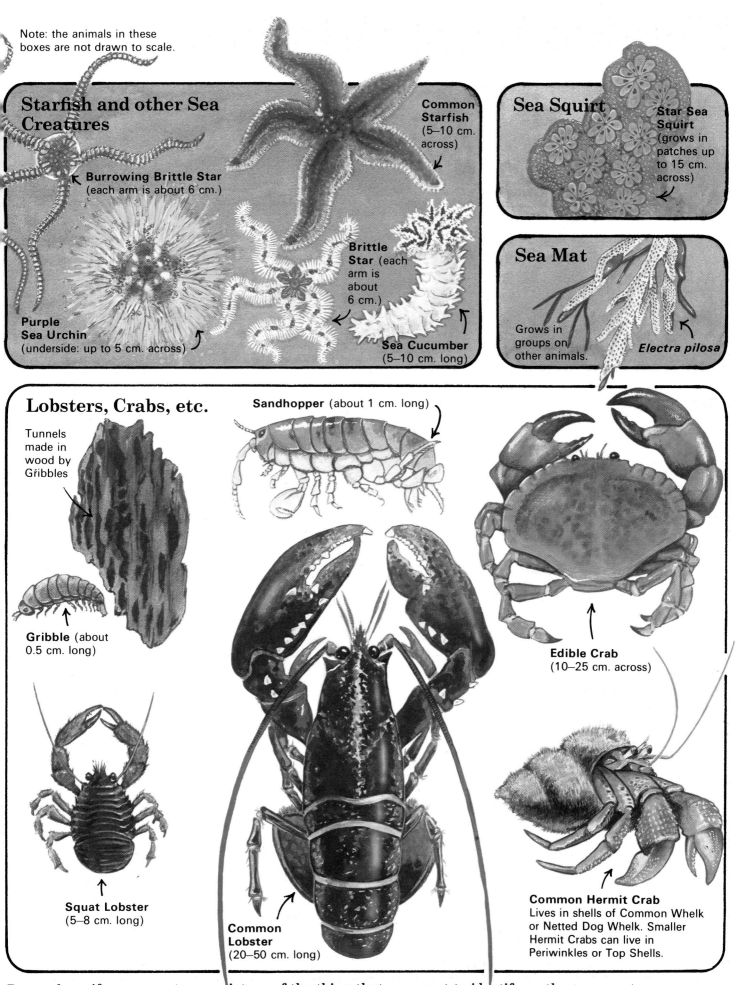

Starfish and other Sea Creatures

Common Starfish (5–10 cm. across)

← **Burrowing Brittle Star** (each arm is about 6 cm.)

Brittle Star (each arm is about 6 cm.)

Purple Sea Urchin (underside: up to 5 cm. across)

Sea Cucumber (5–10 cm. long)

Sea Squirt

Star Sea Squirt (grows in patches up to 15 cm. across)

Sea Mat

Grows in groups on other animals.

Electra pilosa

Lobsters, Crabs, etc.

Sandhopper (about 1 cm. long)

Tunnels made in wood by Gribbles

Gribble (about 0.5 cm. long)

Edible Crab (10–25 cm. across)

Squat Lobster (5–8 cm. long)

Common Lobster (20–50 cm. long)

Common Hermit Crab
Lives in shells of Common Whelk or Netted Dog Whelk. Smaller Hermit Crabs can live in Periwinkles or Top Shells.

Remember—if you cannot see a picture of the thing that you want to identify on these pages, turn to the page earlier in the book that deals with that kind of animal or plant.

Snails

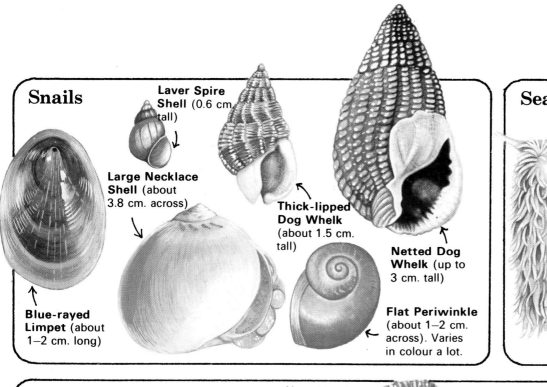

Laver Spire Shell (0.6 cm. tall)

Large Necklace Shell (about 3.8 cm. across)

Thick-lipped Dog Whelk (about 1.5 cm. tall)

Netted Dog Whelk (up to 3 cm. tall)

Blue-rayed Limpet (about 1–2 cm. long)

Flat Periwinkle (about 1–2 cm. across). Varies in colour a lot.

Sea Slugs

Sea Lemon (5–8 cm. long). Shown with ribbons of eggs.

Common Grey Sea Slug (up to 7 cm. long)

Bivalve Shells

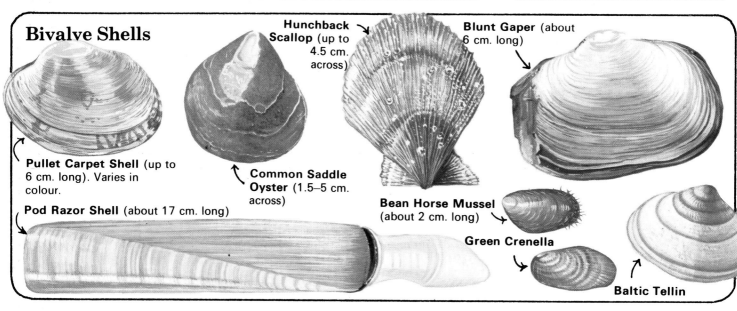

Hunchback Scallop (up to 4.5 cm. across)

Blunt Gaper (about 6 cm. long)

Pullet Carpet Shell (up to 6 cm. long). Varies in colour.

Common Saddle Oyster (1.5–5 cm. across)

Pod Razor Shell (about 17 cm. long)

Bean Horse Mussel (about 2 cm. long)

Green Crenella

Baltic Tellin

Cuttlefish and Octopus

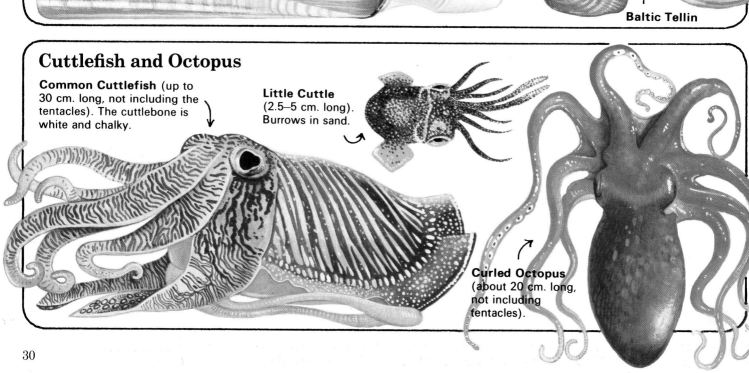

Common Cuttlefish (up to 30 cm. long, not including the tentacles). The cuttlebone is white and chalky.

Little Cuttle (2.5–5 cm. long). Burrows in sand.

Curled Octopus (about 20 cm. long, not including tentacles).

Birds

Fulmar. Nests on cliffs in summer.

Shelduck

Scaup Estuaries and bays in winter.

Common Scoter

Male Female

Eider Duck Rocky and sandy sea coasts.

Grey Plover. Has greyer appearance in winter.

Oyster-catcher Shores, islands, estuaries.

Knot. Has grey plumage in winter.

Sanderling. Has pale plumage in winter.

Curlew Sand dunes and grassy coasts.

Greenshank Marshes, estuaries, and mud flats.

Lesser Black-Backed Gull. Coasts and estuaries. Nests on cliffs.

Male

Stonechat Sea cliffs

Female

Wheatear

Plants

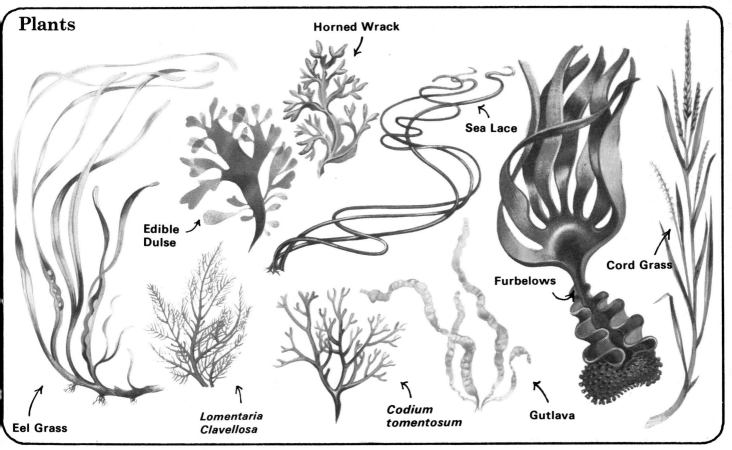

Horned Wrack

Sea Lace

Edible Dulse

Furbelows

Cord Grass

Eel Grass

Lomentaria Clavellosa

Codium tomentosum

Gutlava

Remember—if you cannot see a picture of the thing that you want to identify on these pages, turn to the page earlier in the book that deals with that kind of animal or plant.

Near the Seashore

Whales and dolphins

Dolphins and porpoises are small whales. You may see whales near the coast, and dolphins when they leap out of the water.

Whales are mammals, and have a blow-hole on top of their heads for breathing air. You may see a "spout" or "blow" from a whale; this is when it comes to the surface to breathe out. It blows out not water, but moist air. The moisture condenses when it meets the cold air, and forms a jet of droplets.

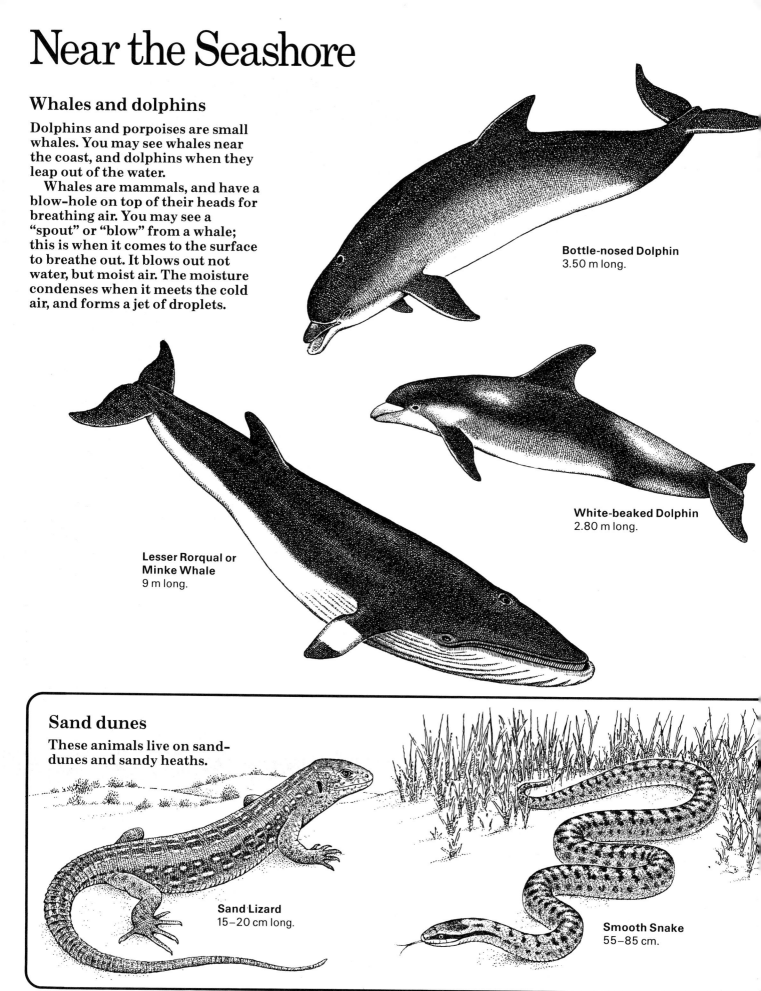

Bottle-nosed Dolphin
3.50 m long.

White-beaked Dolphin
2.80 m long.

Lesser Rorqual or Minke Whale
9 m long.

Sand dunes

These animals live on sand-dunes and sandy heaths.

Sand Lizard
15–20 cm long.

Smooth Snake
55–85 cm.

Common Dolphin
2.20 m long.

Common Porpoise
1.60 m long.

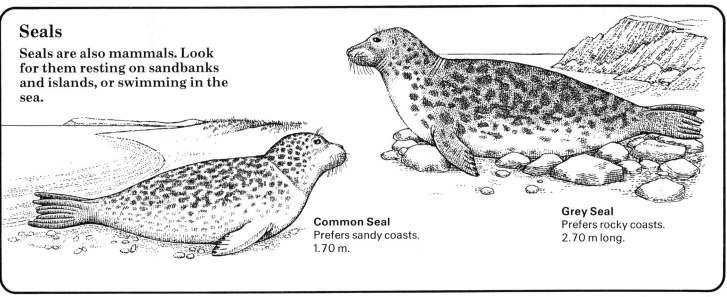

Seals

Seals are also mammals. Look for them resting on sandbanks and islands, or swimming in the sea.

Common Seal
Prefers sandy coasts.
1.70 m.

Grey Seal
Prefers rocky coasts.
2.70 m long.

Natterjack Toad
Rare. 6–8 cm.

Rabbit
Body length 40 cm.

Long-eared Bat

Stoat

Part 2 written by
Rosemary Hartill

Consultant Editor
Alfred Leutscher, B.Sc., F.Z.S.

Fox

Part 2 WILD ANIMALS

This section is about European mammals. A mammal is a warm-blooded creature, which means that its body temperature does not vary very much. Nearly all mammals give birth to live young, who suckle milk from their mother. Most mammals are covered in fur or hair. Look on pages 64-5 for more about mammals if you are not sure what they are.

This section tells you where and how mammals live, and how to find them. It shows you pictures of their tracks, and describes lots of other signs and clues you can look for.

The most common mammals are shown, along with a few rarer ones. The charts on pages 60-63 are a good source for quick reference if you want to identify an animal you have seen. If you can't see a picture of it there, look on other pages in this section that deal with the kind of animal you saw.

As well as spotting animals, this section tells you how to do lots of projects, like building a hide, so that you can watch mammals more easily. It also gives you ideas for making collections, and gathering information in the form of maps, plaster casts and drawings.

Roe Deer

How to start

Most mammals live in the country, but some, like certain kinds of rats and mice, live in towns. You can see mammals in different places— badgers live in woods, hares on farmland, otters on river banks and seals by the sea. Rabbits, squirrels and deer can be seen in town parks. Hedgehogs and foxes are common in and on the outskirts of towns.

Mammals are shy and frightened of people, so the best places to look for them are quiet, hidden spots like holes, ditches, trees and hedges. The animals' sharp senses will detect you unless you move slowly and quietly.

When to look

The best times to look for mammals are at dawn and dusk when many leave their homes to search for food. All mammals leave signs behind them—look for these at any time.

Spring and summer are good times to see mammals and their young. It is more difficult to see them in autumn and winter, but look for their food stores in autumn, and for tracks in the snow in winter.

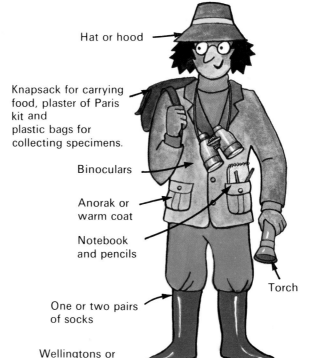

Hat or hood

Knapsack for carrying food, plaster of Paris kit and plastic bags for collecting specimens.

Binoculars

Anorak or warm coat

Notebook and pencils

Torch

One or two pairs of socks

Wellingtons or strong shoes

What to wear

When you go out on a field trip to watch mammals, you will have to sit still for some time. Wrap up well. Wear dull coloured clothes so that you blend in with the background. Take something to eat, but don't pack food in paper bags that rustle. The noise would startle the animals.

If you want to watch mammals at night, use a torch with red cellophane over the beam. The red light will not disturb the animals.

Making notes

It is hard to remember everything you see, so make notes as you go along, marking down exactly where you find any specimens that you decide to take home or signs that you spot. Draw tracks carefully so that you can identify them later.

Torch to use at night

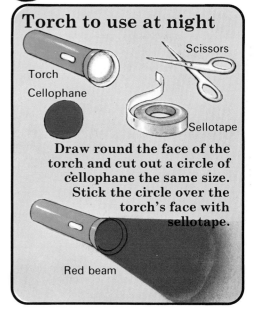

Torch

Cellophane

Scissors

Sellotape

Draw round the face of the torch and cut out a circle of cellophane the same size. Stick the circle over the torch's face with sellotape.

Red beam

What to look for

Tracks and runs

Look for mammal tracks in mud, sand or snow and after rain when the ground is soft. If you lose a trail, search in a circle around it (as shown above) until you find it again. Well-worn trails, or runs, may lead to a mammal's home.

Homes

Mammal homes can be on the ground, below it or above it. Piles of earth, dropped bedding or flattened vegetation are all signs that a home may be nearby.

Hair and droppings

Hairs are a good clue towards discovering which mammals live in a particular area. Look also at the size, shape, colour and position of droppings.

Meal remains

Look for half-eaten cones, nuts, vegetables and dead animals and birds. These may have tell-tale signs showing you which mammal has been eating them.

Damage

Many mammals damage trees and shrubs by feeding, rubbing or scratching. The position of these marks will help you to identify the mammal.

Making a map

Make a map like this one of an area near your house and mark on it the animals and animal signs that you see there. Some animals are more difficult to see than others, but you may find droppings and feeding signs to give you clues. Include paths, hedges, fences, streams and ponds on your map.

Over several months you can build up a picture of where animals live and hunt in your area. The picture below shows some of the animals you might spot. Red Squirrels are rare in Britain, but are more common in other parts of Europe.

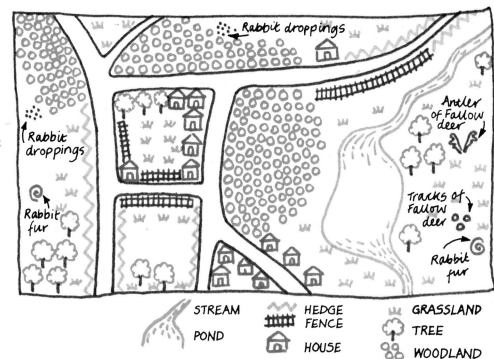

Rabbit droppings

Rabbit droppings

Rabbit fur

Antler of Fallow deer

Tracks of Fallow deer

Rabbit fur

STREAM
POND

HEDGE
FENCE
HOUSE

GRASSLAND
TREE
WOODLAND

Red Squirrel

Fallow Deer

Hedgehog

Rabbits

Wood Mouse

How to watch mammals

You need patience and some knowledge of a mammal's habits to catch more than a glimpse of it. Find out first where it lives, what it eats and when it is awake. Some small mammals are hard to find because they live underground. It is easier to watch larger mammals, but only when you have learnt to overcome their very good sense of smell. Be careful that the wind does not carry your scent to the mammal.

If you decide to build a hide, ask the landowner for permission before you start.

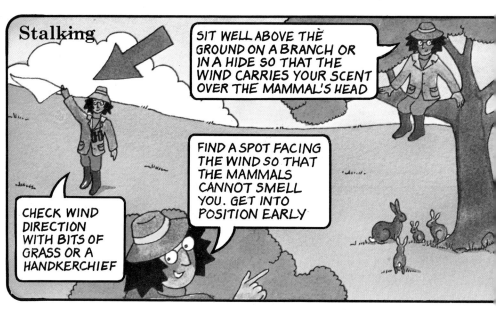

Stalking

SIT WELL ABOVE THE GROUND ON A BRANCH OR IN A HIDE SO THAT THE WIND CARRIES YOUR SCENT OVER THE MAMMAL'S HEAD

FIND A SPOT FACING THE WIND SO THAT THE MAMMALS CANNOT SMELL YOU. GET INTO POSITION EARLY

CHECK WIND DIRECTION WITH BITS OF GRASS OR A HANDKERCHIEF

Wigwam

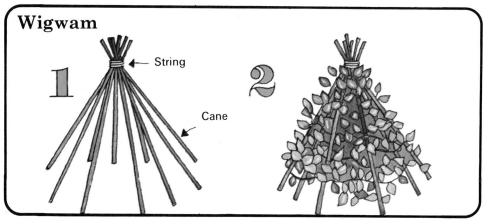

String

Cane

When you find a good place to see mammals, try building a simple hide to watch them from. Make a wigwam frame big enough to sit in from thin branches or bamboo

canes. Tie the tops together with string. Weave leafy twigs on to the canes. You may have to stay quietly inside for some hours, but it should be well worth the wait.

Tent

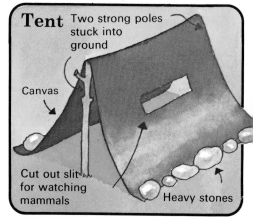

Two strong poles stuck into ground

Canvas

Cut out slit for watching mammals

Heavy stones

Make a simple tent using dull green or brown canvas or other heavy material. Hold the edges down with stones. Remember to wear dull-coloured clothes.

Tree platform

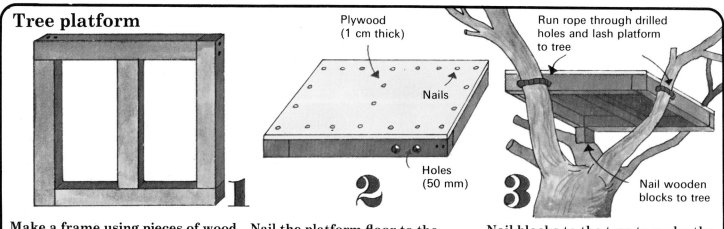

Plywood (1 cm thick)

Nails

Holes (50 mm)

Run rope through drilled holes and lash platform to tree

Nail wooden blocks to tree

Make a frame using pieces of wood 5 cm x 7.5 cm. Nail the joints together. The size and shape of the frame will depend on the tree.

Nail the platform floor to the frame. Drill pairs of holes where the frame will touch the branches.

Nail blocks to the tree to make the platform level. Tie the platform to the tree firmly. Make sure it is safe and secure before you use it.

Facing the wind

WHEN YOU SPOT A MAMMAL MOVE AROUND QUIETLY IN A WIDE CIRCLE UNTIL THE WIND IS BLOWING IN YOUR FACE. KEEP OUT OF SIGHT.

WHEN THERE IS NO COVER, CRAWL OR SLIDE NEARER TO THE MAMMAL ON YOUR STOMACH. FREEZE IF IT LOOKS UP

IF YOU ARE STALKING A DEER AND STILL CANNOT GET CLOSE ENOUGH, WAVE A WHITE HANDKERCHIEF ON A STICK. STAY HIDDEN. THE DEER MAY GET CURIOUS AND MOVE CLOSER

Baiting

Squirrels like nuts, raisins and chocolate

If you think you know where a mammal lives, try putting some food near its home. Hide and wait for the mammal to come out.

Stoats and Weasels like dead birds and mice, eggs and raw meat

To attract a Stoat or Weasel, put bait in some kind of tunnel (like a length of drainpipe) or in an arch made of stones.

Making plaster casts of tracks

If you find a good clear track, you can make a plaster cast of it.

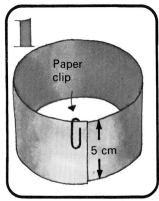

1 Paper clip 5 cm

Bend a strip of strong card (30 cm long) into a circle and join the ends together.

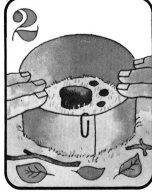

2

Remove leaves and bits of twig. Push the card ring into the ground.

3 Plastic spoon — Plastic bowl

Put some water in a bowl. Sprinkle plaster of Paris up to same level. Stir to a paste.

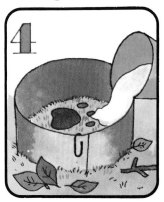

4

Pour the paste in the ring near the edge. Tap the ring to remove any air bubbles.

5

When set (20 minutes), lift up the cast with a knife. Gently remove the ring.

6 Paint

Clean the finished cast under a tap. You can paint it and give it a coat of clear varnish.

Badgers

Badgers are common in Britain, especially in hilly, wooded country. They are nocturnal animals, which means that they hunt, eat and play at night. During the day they rest in their underground homes, called setts. This is the best time to look for the sett entrance, using the clues shown on these pages. Go back to watch the Badgers come out in the evening, preferably taking an adult with you.

Badgers have poor eyesight, but their senses of smell and hearing are very sharp. You should get into position, facing the wind, about an hour before sunset so that your arrival doesn't frighten them. Wear warm, dark clothes and wait patiently.

Footprints in the sand

To check if a sett is being used, put some wet sand round the entrance and smooth it. Put down twigs too. Look next day for tracks and check to see if the twigs have been disturbed. When Badgers walk, the hind foot steps into the track left by the fore foot.

Look for hairs at the sett entrance. Badgers often pause here to scratch and groom their fur. They moult during the summer.

Notice the scratch marks on the tree trunk. The Badgers have made these with their claws.

Torn-up tufts of grass are a sign that a Badger has been trying to get at an insect at the grass roots.
Patches of flattened undergrowth show where Badgers play.

Badgers eat earthworms, Rabbits, fruit, small rodents and wasp nests. The remains of wasp and bee nests are left spread out on the ground like this.

40

If you follow a Badger path out of a wood and into a field, you may find Badger hairs caught on barbed wire.

If a path near the sett leads under low branches or fallen trees, it is a Badger run. It may lead to a stream or to another sett entrance.

Badgers rub their fur and clean their claws on trees. Look for scratch marks, dirt and hairs on tree bark.

This furrow has been made by Badgers moving soil away from the sett entrance.

The sett

Ventilation hole

Entrance

Mound of earth

Sleeping chambers

Breeding chamber

Look for hay, bracken, dry leaves and moss near the sett. This is bedding material dropped by the Badger as it drags the foliage backwards into the sett.

Setts can be dug as long as 20 metres and are often on more than one level with several entrances. Sometimes Badgers share the sett with Foxes. Every winter the Badgers clean out their sett.

Badgers are clean, tidy animals and always use special holes outside the sett as dung pits. The droppings can be liquid, or dry and sausage-shaped.

41

Stoats and Weasels

When you go for a country walk, you may be lucky enough to see a Stoat or a Weasel. They are mainly nocturnal, but you may see them during the day. These animals are carnivores, which means that they eat other animals. They hunt mostly by scent and hearing, rather than sight, so keep quite still if you see one—it may not notice you. Stoats and Weasels are very inquisitive and sit up on their hind legs to look around.

The other animals on these pages are closely related to Stoats and Weasels.

Spot the difference

Stoat

Weasel

IF YOU ARE NOT SURE WHETHER YOU ARE SEEING A STOAT OR A WEASEL, LOOK AT THE ANIMAL'S TAIL. A STOAT'S TAIL HAS A BLACK TIP. STOATS ARE LARGER THAN WEASELS

Tracks

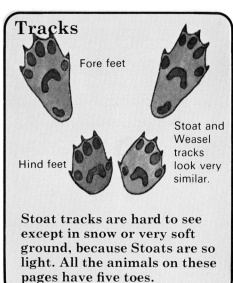

Fore feet

Hind feet

Stoat and Weasel tracks look very similar.

Stoat tracks are hard to see except in snow or very soft ground, because Stoats are so light. All the animals on these pages have five toes.

Hunting

Stoats and Weasels both attack animals larger than themselves. Rabbits are so frightened of Stoats that they become dazed. The Stoat then leaps and attacks the Rabbit with its sharp teeth. If you find a dead Rabbit with the back of the head gnawed away, you may have disturbed a Stoat at a meal.

Stoat in winter

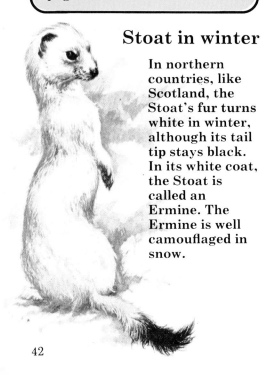

In northern countries, like Scotland, the Stoat's fur turns white in winter, although its tail tip stays black. In its white coat, the Stoat is called an Ermine. The Ermine is well camouflaged in snow.

Weasels

Weasels are long and slender and can easily crawl down small holes or into cracks in walls or rocks. They can follow mice and voles into their burrows to catch them, and will sometimes sleep in their victim's hole after the meal. Like Stoats, Weasels hunt in family groups, called packs.

Martens

Stoats and Weasels are quite common, but if you see a marten you will be very lucky indeed. The only species in Britain is the shy Pine Marten which is now very rare and lives only in remote mountain areas. Both Pine and Beech Martens live in other parts of Europe and in Asia.

Pine Martens

Pine Martens live in or near trees, including pines. They are expert climbers and can even catch squirrels. At night they will sleep in a tree hollow, a rocky crevice or sometimes in a magpie's nest.

Yellow bib

Wood Mouse

Beech Martens

As they like rocky places, Beech Martens are sometimes called Stone Martens. Their fur is greyer than the Pine Marten's and they have a white bib on their front.

To open eggs, martens bite an oblong, almost rectangular hole in the shell.

Feeding

As well as eating squirrels, mice, insects and berries, martens also raid hen-houses, bee hives and pigeon lofts for food. Beech Martens often live near farms where these things can be found. Dead birds, egg shells, Hedgehog spines and skins or droppings in a loft or shed are all signs that a Beech Marten has been there.

European Mink

Minks

Mink live near streams and marshes and swim well. They eat fishes, water birds and frogs and, like Polecats, kill far more than they need. The European Mink does not live in Britain, but wild American minks, which have escaped from fur farms, are a common pest.

Polecats

Polecats like wooded, hilly country. They are now rare in Britain. They have scent glands which smell strongly. Sometimes they store live frogs for the winter, first paralysing the frog with a bite and then pushing it into a burrow until it is needed.

Foxes

Foxes are more difficult to watch than Badgers—they travel further and change their homes more often. They live in all sorts of places, from woodland to moorland. Some now live in towns.

The best time to see Foxes is in May and June when the cubs are young and playful and when the adults still bring them food.

A Fox's home, called an earth, is often an old Rabbit burrow made larger, or a Badger sett. You can smell the Fox's musty scent around the entrance if the earth is occupied. Watch from a tree in the early morning or evening.

Tracks

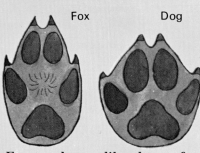

Fox   Dog

Fox tracks are like those of a dog, but the claw marks are slimmer and more pointed and there is a much wider space between the marks of the front and back pads.

Droppings

Fox droppings are sausage-shaped, with a spirally twisted point at one end. They vary in colour from black to grey depending on what the Fox has been eating.

Growing up

Foxes sometimes bury food and return to collect it later. These cubs are digging up food buried by their mother.

When the cubs are six weeks old, they play outside the earth, fighting over food the vixen brings them. Look for reddish hairs and the remains of meals. You may see bones, feathers and Rabbits' feet.

Cubs are usually born in March or April. For the first four weeks they are suckled by the female, called a vixen, in the earth. The male or dog Fox leaves food outside for her, but he does not help her care for the cubs.

Feeding

By summer the cubs are beginning to hunt alone. Their mother has taught them how to catch animals, like voles, mice, insects and squirrels, by springing into the air and pouncing.

To catch an earthworm, a Fox carefully watches to detect its exact position. Then the Fox stabs its nose downwards and grabs.

Young Foxes often hunt near Rabbit warrens, hoping to surprise a weak or sickly Rabbit. Like Stoats, Foxes may jump and somersault to attract their prey.

Foxes may scavenge in rubbish dumps, looking for bones and other scraps. Fruits, like blackberries, are also welcome food for a hungry Fox.

Under cover of night, Foxes may attack farm poultry. You may find hens, ducks or pheasants abandoned by Foxes. They usually bite the bird's head off.

Foxes will also scavenge for food in dustbins, even though this means taking the risk of approaching houses.

Winter

In winter, food is scarce and adult Foxes may protect their own food supply and territory by driving young Foxes away. Foxes mark their area, or territory, by leaving their strongly scented droppings on the ground, or on little hillocks or tree stumps.

Winter is the mating season and the time when dog Foxes establish their territory and when vixens prepare the earth for the cubs. These Foxes will have a family of their own in the spring.

Otters

Otters live by rivers and the sea. They are nocturnal and wander long distances at night. During the day they rest in their well-hidden nests, called holts. These are made in hollow trees or at the end of tunnels in river banks, sometimes with an underwater entrance.

At night Otters are easily disturbed, but quiet daytime visits to look for signs will not worry them. Wait for Otters on a bridge where they are used to seeing people. Listen for the Otter's soft clear whistle.

Signs and tracks

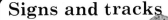

Otters live mainly on fish, as well as eating shellfish, water birds and frogs. You may see fish bones and crab shells on the river bank or seashore.

Otters' droppings, called spraints, are black, slimy and smelly. Old ones are white and crumbly. They are usually left in obvious places, like the top of a tree stump, where they act as "keep out" signs to other Otters.

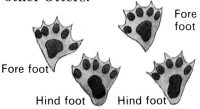

Fore foot

Fore foot

Hind foot   Hind foot

Each Otter's foot has five toes joined by a web. In deep snow the tracks often appear with a furrow between them made by the Otter's body.

Look for Otter slides like this one down muddy banks into water, or in sand dunes or snow.

Otters are very playful animals. You can sometimes see them leaping in and out of the water just for fun.

Otters swim and dive well using the strong tail as a rudder and the front legs for steering and balance. Otter fur is waterproof.

The position of the eyes, ears and nose allow the Otter to breathe and look round without lifting its head too much when swimming.

A line of bubbles like this is a sign that an Otter may be swimming beneath the surface.

Cubs have to be taught to go into the water, but they immediately know how to swim. As soon as they have learnt to hunt, the male, or dog, leaves them. The female, or bitch, stays with them for some months.

Under water, the ears and nostrils close to stop water entering.

Bats

Look for bats in the evening when they hunt for insects, especially near lakes and streams and in woodland.

Bats are the only mammals that can fly. Their finger bones are very long, and skin is stretched over them to make a wing, which is attached to the hind leg. When bats fly, they spread their hind legs to keep their wings open. Most European bats also have skin that stretches between their legs, enclosing the tail. This skin can be formed into a pouch for catching flying insects.

Hunting in the dark

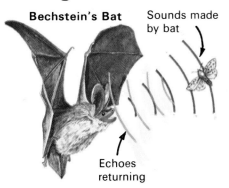

Bechstein's Bat

Sounds made by bat

Echoes returning

Bats rely on their sharp hearing to hunt in the dark. They make high-pitched noises as they fly. From the returning echoes, bats can tell the exact position of flying insects.

Roosting and hibernation

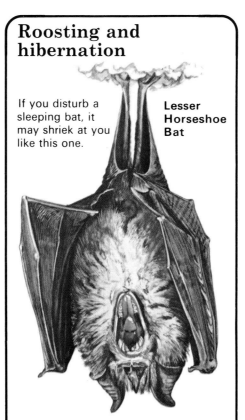

If you disturb a sleeping bat, it may shriek at you like this one.

Lesser Horseshoe Bat

Most bats sleep during the day, hanging by their claws in a quiet, dark roost. From October until March, bats hibernate. They sleep in hollow trees, caves, old mines or lofts, but they dislike dust and cobwebs and may choose quite new buildings. If you find bats hibernating, don't disturb them—they may die.

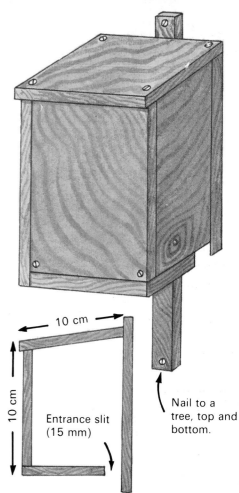

10 cm

10 cm

Entrance slit (15 mm)

Nail to a tree, top and bottom.

Making a bat box

You can attract bats to your garden with a bat box like this. Use thick, rough, untreated wood so that the bats can get a grip on the surfaces. The small entrance slit prevents squirrels or birds from moving into the box. Attach it to a tree at least 1.5 metres from the ground. You may have to try putting your box in different positions before bats use it.

Greater Horseshoe Bats

Horseshoe bats get their name from the shape of the fleshy part of the nose called the "nose-leaf". The Greater Horseshoe Bat flies very low and picks up insects from the ground as well as in the air.

Pipistrelles

The Pipistrelle is the most common British bat as well as the smallest bat in Europe.

You may see these bats in towns, flying round street lamps, as well as in the country. Their flight is quick and jerky. However, it is almost impossible to identify a particular species of bat in flight, because they all look very similar in the dark. If you can examine one closely, 'its size and the shape of its face and ears will help you to identify it.

Hedgehogs, Moles and Shrews

Hedgehogs

Hedgehogs are common, and are one of the easiest mammals to watch. You are most likely to see one at night, trundling across a field or lane, or under a hedge. Look in gardens and churchyards.

Hedgehogs grunt and snuffle and sometimes squeal loudly. Listen for the loud rustling of leaves in ditches.

When frightened, a Hedgehog rolls itself into a tight ball with its prickles sticking up. Many are killed by cars, and you may find their bodies on roads. In winter, hibernating Hedgehogs often die when rubbish dumps and piles of leaves are burnt.

Strange behaviour

Hedgehogs sometimes roll on fruit and carry it away on their spines. It is possible that they do it on purpose, but this seems unlikely.

Hedgehogs climb well and can get over high fences. If they fall from a height, they land on their spines which act as a cushion so that they do not hurt themselves.

Hedgehogs hibernate from late October to March in a nest of grass, moss and leaves. They curl up like this to sleep.

Try tempting Hedgehogs to your garden each night by leaving out some water and dog or cat food.

Moles

Moles live almost anywhere where the soil is soft enough to dig and where earthworms are plentiful. They can be found in farmland, parks and football fields, where they are a pest. Moles live alone and spend most of their time underground. They are mainly nocturnal, but they sometimes appear during the day. Look for them in spring in the breeding season when males chase one another. You may see one drinking in a ditch, or looking for earthworms after heavy rain.

Moles have soft grey-black, velvety fur which lies smoothly in any direction. The snout is pink and very sensitive. Their front legs are short and powerful with shovel-shaped feet which are used for digging. Moles hear well, but their small eyes are often hidden by fur and sometimes by skin.

All these mammals are insectivores, which means that they live mainly on insects. They also eat slugs and earthworms, and Hedgehogs will eat frogs, birds' eggs and even Adders.

They all need to eat a lot to survive and so they spend most of their time searching for food.

> Baby Hedgehogs are born naked and blind. Their spines are soft at first, but when they have hardened, they are sharp. Be careful handling Hedgehogs. Fleas live on their bodies, close to the spines.

> A female Hedgehog is called a sow, and the male is known as a boar.

Shrews

Common Shrew

Common Shrews and Pygmy Shrews live in thick undergrowth in fields, woods, hedgerows and ditches. They eat beetles, slugs and worms, above and below the ground, and some plants.

You can tell a shrew from a mouse by its long, twitching, whiskery snout.

Shrews have a musky smell and, perhaps for this reason, their bodies are rarely eaten by predators.

Water Shrews

Air bubbles caught in the fur make Water Shrews look silvery under water.

Water Shrews live along the banks of streams, rivers and lakes. Most of their day is spent sleeping or looking for food. They eat gnats, beetles, snails, worms and small fishes.

Water Shrews swim well and if you disturb one you will hear the splash as it jumps into the water.

Molehill

Fortress

Nest

The fortress may have a larder where worms are stored.

Exit tunnels lead to the surface at an angle.

A sure sign of Moles is a series of small heaps of earth called molehills. These are made by Moles pushing surplus soil out from their burrows. If the earth is fresh, the molehill is new. Older ones have grass growing on them.

An extra-large molehill is called a fortress. Inside is a nest for sleeping lined with dead leaves, moss and grass. A smaller fortress is used for breeding.

Burrows are so narrow that a Mole's fur is squeezed clean as it travels through. Hunting burrows are deeper.

Rats, Mice and Voles

Common Rats and House Mice live in colonies in all sorts of places close to people. Look for signs of them in warehouses, barns, rubbish dumps, haystacks, by canals, in offices and homes. They breed very fast, eat almost anything, do great damage and spread disease.

House Mice have been known to survive in cold stores by feeding on frozen food. These mice grow special thick coats to keep themselves warm.

Rats, mice and voles are all rodents. Their teeth are specially adapted for gnawing.

Ship Rats

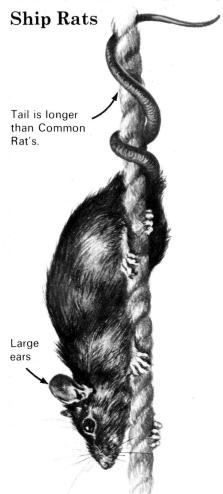

Tail is longer than Common Rat's.

Large ears

Ship Rats are so called because they are usually found on ships or in dock areas. They are also called Black Rats, though not all of them are black. They are very good at climbing.

Look for droppings, half-eaten food, tooth marks and holes in wood, metal and plastic. Listen for squeaking and rustling sounds.

House Mice

Nests are made of old bits of shredded rope, paper, rags and grass and are usually hidden, except if the building is completely neglected by people.

Dirt smears like this are made by rats rubbing their greasy coats against objects as they pass by.

Lead pipe gnawed by Common Rat.

Common Rat

Common Rats are also called Brown Rats, although some of them are black.

Harvest Mice

Harvest Mice are the smallest mice in Europe. They live in fields, reed beds and tall grasses. They use their tails as an extra limb when climbing.

Wood Mice

Wood Mice, or Field Mice, are common in the country. You may find their stores of nuts and seeds hidden in old birds' nests, nest boxes and cracks in walls or tree stumps.

Voles

You can tell voles from rats and mice by their blunter faces, small ears and short tails. They are mainly nocturnal and move quickly. Voles are common although they are eaten by many meat-eating animals, such as Foxes and birds of prey.

If you look in undergrowth, you may find vole runs, which will probably lead to burrows. Look for gnawed roots and other feeding signs. Voles damage trees by gnawing bark too—look for their fine tooth marks.

Bank Voles

Long tail

Look in banks and ditches bordering lanes and woods. Bank Voles eat grasses, nuts, buds, shoots, berries and seeds. They are good at swimming and also climb well and will gnaw bark high up in trees.

Field Voles

Short tail

Field Voles live in grassland, heath, dunes and woods. They eat grasses, rushes, bark and clover.

In winter, they make runs under snow, lining them with grass. You can see these tunnels when snow has melted.

Water Voles attack crops like turnips from below. They eat the whole turnip before starting on the next one.

Water Voles swim with only their noses showing above the water.

Broken bits of plant are piled up ready to eat.

Water Voles

Water Voles live on the edges of streams, small ponds and canals. Approach quietly and you may see one on the bank grooming its fur. If frightened, it will dive into the water and may stay under for over 30 seconds before it comes up in the safety of a tunnel in the bank, or perhaps behind a water lily or some rushes. Look for the tunnels in banks close to the water's edge.

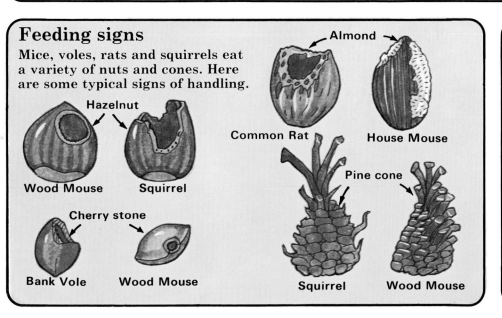

Feeding signs

Mice, voles, rats and squirrels eat a variety of nuts and cones. Here are some typical signs of handling.

Hazelnut

Wood Mouse

Squirrel

Almond

Common Rat

House Mouse

Cherry stone

Bank Vole

Wood Mouse

Pine cone

Squirrel

Wood Mouse

Lemmings

Snowy Owl

Norway Lemming

Norway Lemmings live in Scandinavia. They are strong burrowers and breed very fast. Many are eaten by Snowy Owls and Arctic Foxes.

Squirrels and Dormice

Red Squirrels

Most Red Squirrels live in forests of coniferous trees, like pine and fir, in remote areas. If you find any of the signs shown on the opposite page, leave pieces of chocolate, nuts or raisins nearby (perhaps on a tree stump) and settle into a comfortable hiding place to wait. Early morning is a good time.

Although squirrels will dart away if you disturb them, they will often come back to have another look at you. Keep still and you may see an excited squirrel chattering at you from a safe place in the tree above.

Squirrels have very good eyesight and hearing. They are always twitching their noses and whiskers, ready to sense danger.

Unlike most animals, squirrels can use their forepaws as hands.

The big bushy tail helps the squirrel to balance as it runs along branches and jumps from tree to tree.

Red Squirrels moult their fur twice a year. The softer, longer winter coat keeps them warm in winter.

Squirrels can leap as far as five metres or more between branches.

Grey Squirrels

Grey Squirrels were introduced to Britain from North America and are now more common here than Red Squirrels. They live in city parks and gardens as well as in woodland. When food is scarce in winter, they will sometimes eat out of your hand, but be careful—they may bite.

Baby squirrels are born between April and June and are blind and naked at birth. After seven or eight weeks, they climb out of the drey and begin exploring the tree tops. Use binoculars to watch them closely.

Nests called dreys are about the size of a football. Look in forks of trees and in hollows. They are made of twigs, but the inside may be lined with moss, leaves, fur and feathers. In bad weather squirrels will stay in the drey all day, but they do not hibernate.

Three vertical, parallel scratch marks on bark are made by the squirrel's longest fingers and toes. To see them, you may have to climb the tree. They are usually on the route to the drey.

Squirrels eat seeds, buds, fungi, cones and fruits. They often have a favourite feeding place, such as a tree stump, and they scatter food remains around it.

Squirrels pull off strips of bark to get at the layer beneath.

Sometimes they gnaw away a ring of bark at the base of the tree.

Every autumn, squirrels bury or hide food. Some of it is eaten during the winter, but most is forgotten and lost.

Squirrel tracks nearly always start and end at a tree, and the feet are usually turned out a little.

Droppings are hard to find except in snow.

Dormice

Common Dormouse

Dormice live in woods and scrub. Look for their round summer nests, made of grass and leaves, in creepers. They sometimes use old birds' nests or even nesting boxes.

Edible Dormouse

This large dormouse looks like a squirrel and lives in woods and gardens. It gets very fat before winter hibernation.

Deer

In Britain, deer herds are most common in the Scottish highlands and in woodland parks belonging to country estates.

Deer are shy of strange objects, so hide in a tree or behind a wall or rock to watch them. You can also watch from a parked car. The best times are at dawn and dusk. Always face the wind as deer have a strong sense of smell.

During the rutting or breeding season (usually in the autumn), some deer can be bad-tempered. Approach them with care.

The picture shows you some of the different kinds of deer you may see in Britain and the signs to look for. You will not see all the signs at the same time of year.

Red Deer

The roaring or "belling" of a male Red Deer is very loud. Listen for it at dawn and dusk in the rutting season (Sept–Oct). At this time, the males, or stags, often wallow in mud or peat. A little later, the colour of the coat changes from dark red to brownish grey for the winter months.

In October, the Fallow buck marks out a rutting territory. He tears bushes with his antlers, scrapes the ground with his hooves and marks the area with scent from glands under his eyes. The does visit him here.

Roe Deer kids

Roe Deer kids are born in May or June. This one is about two weeks old. Twins are common and they stay with the doe for up to a year. When alarmed, a kid will crouch down on the ground. Its spotted coat matches its background and makes it difficult for enemies to spot.

Baby Red Deer are called calves, and baby Fallow Deer are known as fawns.

Red Deer

Red Deer tear down twigs and buds from trees up to two metres from the ground. This is a female, called a hind.

Fallow Deer

Antlers

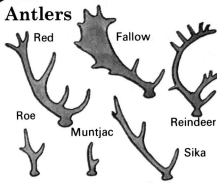

Red   Fallow

Roe   Muntjac   Reindeer

Sika

Every year, most male deer grow and shed (or cast) a pair of antlers. Look for cast, gnawed antlers (usually found singly). The larger the antlers, the older the deer.

Signs

Red   Muntjac   Roe

Sika   Fallow   Reindeer

Deer have cloven (divided) hooves formed from two toes. Reindeer hooves are very broad and deeply cleft, splaying out to support them in snow.

Look for twigs and shoots that have been torn or broken off, gnawed vegetables and bark stripped off trees. These can all be signs of deer.

Red   Roe   Fallow

Deer droppings, called fewmets, are dark brown or black. Look for large piles of them close to feeding places.

While they grow, a deer's antlers are covered with a furry coat called velvet. When growth stops, the velvet begins to strip off. This Sika Deer is helping the process by rubbing (or fraying) its antlers against a young tree. Look for scraped off velvet and marks on tree trunks.

Sika Deer

Deer have no fixed homes, but they do rest in temporary lairs. Look for flattened vegetation and loose leaves, or twigs that have been scraped away.

Roe Deer

Roe rings like this were once called fairy rings. They are made by a male Roe Deer, called a buck, chasing a female, called a doe, in a circle. They do this during the Roe Deers' rutting season in July and August.

Rabbits

You can see Rabbits in almost every type of countryside, especially on commons, sand dunes and in woodland. Rabbits live together in groups of burrows called warrens. They usually come out at dawn and dusk, but you may see them at any time.

Rabbit populations increase very quickly. Each female (called a doe) has an average of ten babies each year. The young become adults within three or four months and they then begin to breed themselves.

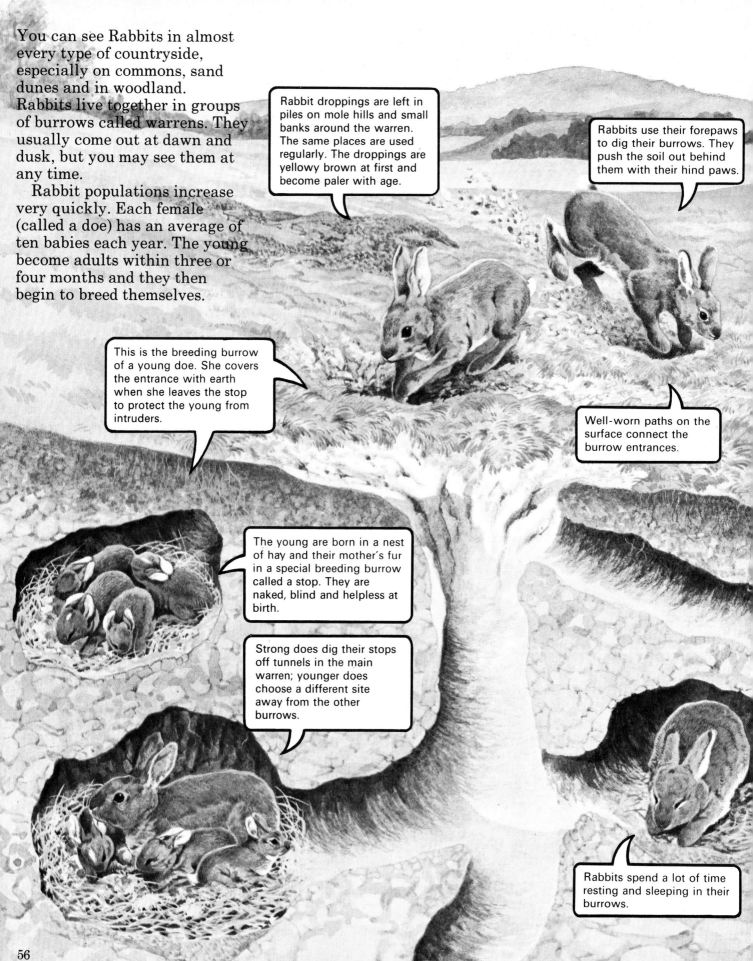

Rabbit droppings are left in piles on mole hills and small banks around the warren. The same places are used regularly. The droppings are yellowy brown at first and become paler with age.

Rabbits use their forepaws to dig their burrows. They push the soil out behind them with their hind paws.

This is the breeding burrow of a young doe. She covers the entrance with earth when she leaves the stop to protect the young from intruders.

Well-worn paths on the surface connect the burrow entrances.

The young are born in a nest of hay and their mother's fur in a special breeding burrow called a stop. They are naked, blind and helpless at birth.

Strong does dig their stops off tunnels in the main warren; younger does choose a different site away from the other burrows.

Rabbits spend a lot of time resting and sleeping in their burrows.

Rabbits are eaten by birds of prey, Foxes, Stoats and Weasels. They can only defend themselves by kicking with their strong hind legs, but usually they run away.

Buzzard

Male rabbits, called bucks, moult between July and September. Look for their hairs caught in hedges and fences.

If alarmed or curious, Rabbits sit up and look around, moving their ears to pick up every sound. When really frightened, they thump their hind feet on the ground and raise their white tails to warn others. Then they bolt for the nearest hole.

Rabbits are sometimes called ''landscape gardeners'' because the plants they like to eat disappear from the area round the warren. New plants, which Rabbits don't like, grow in their place.

This Rabbit is grooming its fur. Rabbits use their front paws and tongues to keep their fur clean.

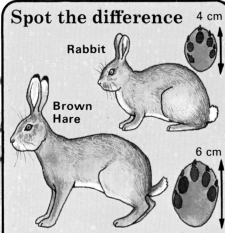

Spot the difference

Rabbit

Brown Hare

4 cm

6 cm

Although Rabbits and Hares look a bit alike, they are easy to tell apart. Hares are bigger, have longer ears with black tips, longer hind legs and are usually solitary. Their tracks are larger too.

Food

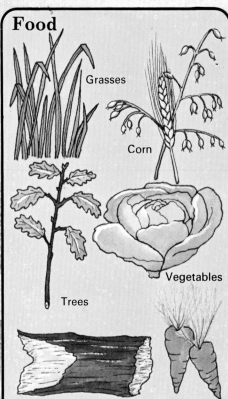

Grasses

Corn

Vegetables

Trees

Rabbits eat grasses, corn crops, root vegetables and young trees. Look for marks of grazing on crops along the edges of fields, and for damage to plants in nurseries and gardens.

Rabbits feed on trees up to 60 cm from the ground. Look for nibbled bark and tooth marks on branches, buds and fruits.

Hares

Look for Brown Hares on farmland, moors, dunes and in woodland. They feed mostly at night and live alone, except during the breeding season. You may see a female, called a doe, resting in her form. The form is a hiding place hollowed out of soft grass where the Hare spends the day resting. She will dash away if you come close, zigzagging to put you off her trail.

The fore feet touch the ground first. Then the hind feet land just in front of the fore feet.

Tracks

The soles of a hare's feet are covered with hairs, so tracks are difficult to see on a firm surface although the claws leave a mark.

A hare's trail is easy to identify in snow or on soft ground. You can tell how fast the hare was moving by the spacing of the tracks.

Fore foot

Hind foot

Mad March Hares

In February and March, hares gather to mate. Males leap and kick, chase in circles and box each other.

Leverets

Baby hares, called leverets, are born with fur and with their eyes open. The doe leaves them alone in a form and visits them regularly to suckle them. If you find leverets, do not disturb them.

Feeding

Hares live mainly on grasses, but they also damage fruit trees and vegetables, particularly in winter. Look for the marks of their sharp, curved front teeth in chewed swedes and turnips and on tree bark. They also bite shoots from young trees.

Droppings

Hares' droppings look like those of Rabbits, but they are larger and a bit flattened. They are yellow brown and quite dry. You can see the plant matter that the hare has eaten.

Blue Hares

The Blue or Mountain Hare lives in the north and in Ireland. It is smaller than the Brown Hare and its ears are not so long. In winter, the Blue Hare's fur becomes white or blue-grey to camouflage it against snow. It shelters between rocks or in a small burrow.

Summer coat

Winter coat

Seals

Seals are sea animals, although they sometimes swim up rivers. Every year they gather on quiet, remote shores like those of the Faroe Islands, the Hebrides and off Ireland and South Wales to breed.

There are two kinds which are common round our coasts —the Grey Seal which breeds in autumn and usually chooses a rocky coast with caves and cliffs for its rookery (breeding place), and the Common Seal which breeds in June and July and prefers sandy beaches and flat rocks.

Find a comfortable place in some rocks and watch from here. Seals are inquisitive animals, so you could try playing a mouth organ to them. They may come over to find out what's happening!

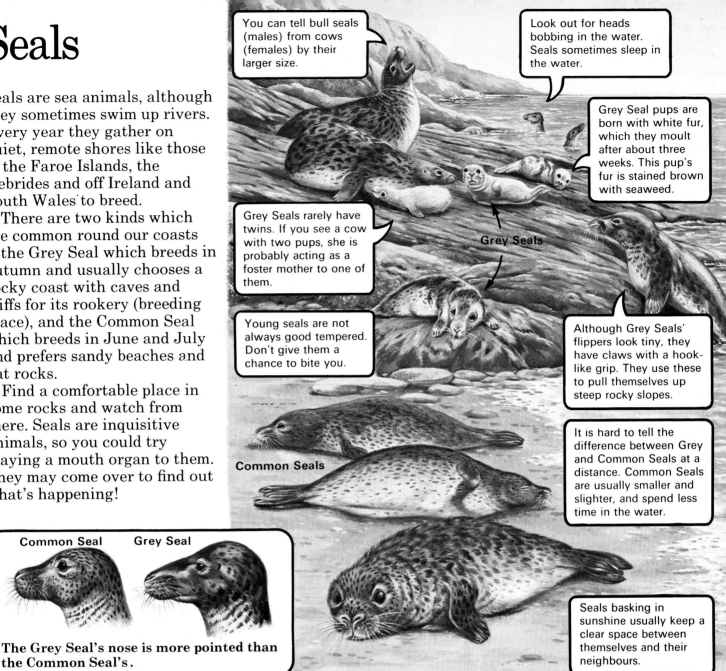

You can tell bull seals (males) from cows (females) by their larger size.

Look out for heads bobbing in the water. Seals sometimes sleep in the water.

Grey Seal pups are born with white fur, which they moult after about three weeks. This pup's fur is stained brown with seaweed.

Grey Seals rarely have twins. If you see a cow with two pups, she is probably acting as a foster mother to one of them.

Grey Seals

Young seals are not always good tempered. Don't give them a chance to bite you.

Although Grey Seals' flippers look tiny, they have claws with a hook-like grip. They use these to pull themselves up steep rocky slopes.

Common Seals

It is hard to tell the difference between Grey and Common Seals at a distance. Common Seals are usually smaller and slighter, and spend less time in the water.

Seals basking in sunshine usually keep a clear space between themselves and their neighbours.

Common Seal   **Grey Seal**

The Grey Seal's nose is more pointed than the Common Seal's.

How a seal moves

Seals are excellent swimmers, but they move in clumsy jerks on land. Their hind flippers only stretch backwards and cannot push. Watch them closely to see how, despite this, they manage to move around.

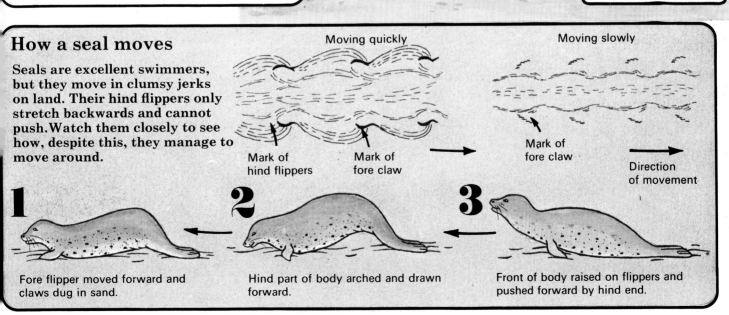

Moving quickly

Moving slowly

Mark of hind flippers   Mark of fore claw   Mark of fore claw

Direction of movement

1 Fore flipper moved forward and claws dug in sand.

2 Hind part of body arched and drawn forward.

3 Front of body raised on flippers and pushed forward by hind end.

More mammals to spot

Meat-eaters

Wild Cat. Thick woods and rocky mountains in Europe, including Scotland. Body 64 cm. Tail 31 cm.

Fore foot

Fore foot

Lynx. Woods on rocky mountainous ground. Not in Britain. Remote parts of Europe. Body 1.5 m. Tail 17 cm.

Pine Marten. Remote woods. Britain's rarest mammal, as many were trapped for fur. Body 47 cm. Tail 24 cm.

Hind foot

Fore foot

Beech Marten. Rocky parts of Europe, often near farms. Not in Britain. Body 45 cm. Tail 24 cm.

Wolf. Woods and mountains in Italy and Norway. Not in Britain. Body 1.2 m. Tail 35 cm.

Hind foot

Bats

Natterer's Bat. Mostly woodland, but also towns. Slow, steady flight. Common in Britain. Body 4.5 cm. Tail 3.5 cm. Arm 3.5 cm.

Daubenton's or Water Bat. Colonies near water. Flies low and fast. Body 4.5 cm. Tail 3.5 cm. Arm 3.5 cm.

Long-eared Bat. Body 4.5 cm. Tail 3.7 cm. Arm 3.7 cm.

Ferret. Tame white Polecat used to hunt rabbits. Some escape and live wild. The descendants of these are often brown and look like wild Polecats. Same size as Polecat.

Hind foot

Polecat. Woods and scrub in Europe. Rare in Britain. Body 38 cm. Tail 24 cm.

Fore foot

Winter

Summer

Fore foot of Arctic Fox

Fore foot of Fox

Arctic Fox. Arctic tundra. Coat changes from brown to white in winter. Body 57 cm. Tail 30 cm.

Brown Bear. Mountains and forests in parts of Europe. Not in Britain. Hibernates. Body 2 m. Tail 10 cm.

Bear's hind foot

Bear's fore foot

Fox. Near woodland or scrub. Common in Britain and found all over Europe. Body 68 cm. Tail 40 cm.

Noctule. Woods and parks. Flies high. Body 7.5 cm. Tail 5 cm. Arm 5 cm.

Whiskered Bat. Near trees. Body ? cm. Tail 4.5 cm. Arm 3.5 cm.

Brown Hare. Farmland and moors. May be more grey in winter. Body 58 cm. Tail 9 cm.

Hind foot   Fore foot

Blue Hare. Moors and woods. Scotland and Ireland. Scottish hare is partly white in winter. Body 50 cm. Tail 6 cm.

Hind foot   Fore foot

Hind foot   Fore foot

Rabbit. Common in woods, moors, dunes, grassland. Body 40 cm. Tail 6 cm.

Shrews

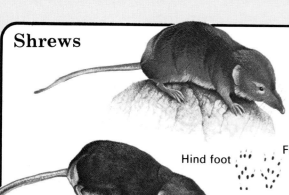

Common Shrew. Found in most of Europe, but not in Ireland. Habitat varies, but likes ground cover. Musky smell. Body 7.5 cm. Tail 4 cm.

Hind foot   Fore foot

Water Shrew. Most of Europe, but not Ireland. Found near water. Swims well. Body 8 cm. Tail 6 cm.

Pygmy Shrew. Found in open woodland, rough grassland and moorland. Britain's smallest mammal. Body 5 cm. Tail 3.5 cm.

Dormice

Edible Dormouse. Large and squirrel-like. Introduced to England, but rare. Woods, gardens, orchards, houses. Body 16 cm. Tail 13 cm.

Hind foot

Fore foot

Garden Dormouse. Not found in Britain. Woods, orchards and gardens in most of Europe. Body 13.5 cm. Tail 10.5 cm.

Common Dormouse. South of England and Wales. Body 7.5 cm. Tail 6.5 cm.

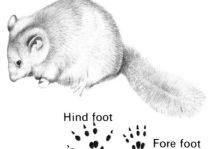

Mice

Wood Mouse. Also called Field Mouse. Fields, hedges, woods, gardens. Body 9.5 cm. Tail 9 cm.

Hind foot   Fore foot

Harvest Mouse. Cornfields, grassland, reed beds. Smallest European rodent. Body 7 cm. Tail 6 cm.

House Mouse. Found all over the world. Houses, fields, woods and other places. Body 9 cm. Tail 8.5 cm.

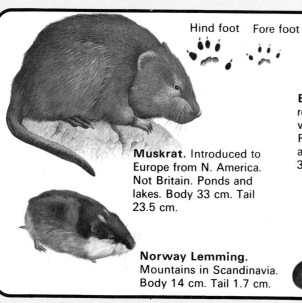

Hind foot   Fore foot

Hind foot   Fore foot

Muskrat. Introduced to Europe from N. America. Not Britain. Ponds and lakes. Body 33 cm. Tail 23.5 cm.

Norway Lemming. Mountains in Scandinavia. Body 14 cm. Tail 1.7 cm.

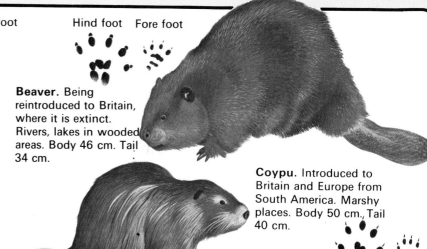

Beaver. Being reintroduced to Britain, where it is extinct. Rivers, lakes in wooded areas. Body 46 cm. Tail 34 cm.

Coypu. Introduced to Britain and Europe from South America. Marshy places. Body 50 cm. Tail 40 cm.

Hind foot   Fore foot

Voles

Water Vole. In or near slow-flowing rivers and lakes. Also grasslands. Body 19 cm. Tail 12 cm.

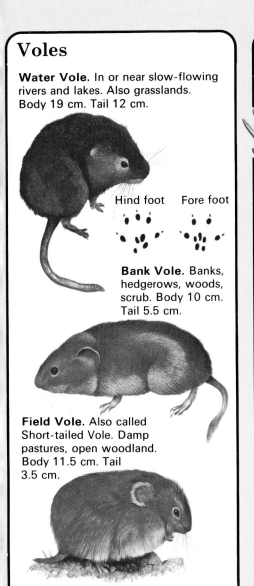

Hind foot   Fore foot

Bank Vole. Banks, hedgerows, woods, scrub. Body 10 cm. Tail 5.5 cm.

Field Vole. Also called Short-tailed Vole. Damp pastures, open woodland. Body 11.5 cm. Tail 3.5 cm.

Hoofed animals

Both male and female Reindeer have antlers.

Fore foot

Elk. USSR and Scandinavia. Not in Britain. 2 m high at shoulder.

Fore foot

Reindeer. North Europe and introduced to Cairngorms in Scotland. 1 m high at shoulder.

Ibex. Wild goat. High rocky mountains in Alps, Spain and Norway. Not in Britain. 75 cm high at shoulder.

Chamois. Alps and Pyrenees. Not in Britain. Wooded and rocky mountains. 75 cm high at shoulder.

Fore foot

Mouflon. Wild sheep. Mountains in Europe. Not in Britain. 70 cm high at shoulder.

Fore foot

Common Rat.

Hind foot

Common Rat. Near people, and woods, banks. Body 24 cm. Tail 20 cm.

Fore foot

Ship Rat. Large ears, long tail. Towns, docks, ships, trees. Body 20 cm. Tail 21 cm.

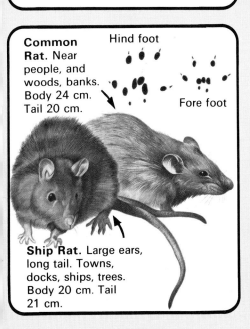

Squirrels

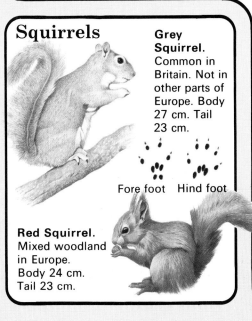

Grey Squirrel. Common in Britain. Not in other parts of Europe. Body 27 cm. Tail 23 cm.

Fore foot   Hind foot

Red Squirrel. Mixed woodland in Europe. Body 24 cm. Tail 23 cm.

Wild Boar. Widespread in woods in Europe. Not in Britain. Young are striped. 90 cm high at shoulder.

Fore foot

More about mammals

People are mammals too.

The **Etruscan Pygmy Shrew** is the smallest ground mammal. Body 4.5 cm. Tail 2.5 cm.

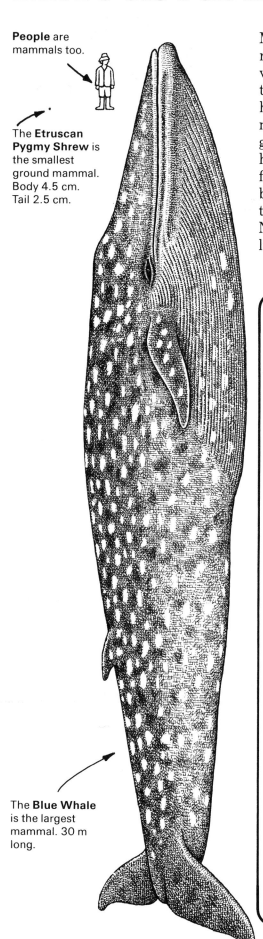

The **Blue Whale** is the largest mammal. 30 m long.

Mammals, like fishes, birds, reptiles and amphibians, are vertebrates, which means that they have a backbone. Mammals have other features which make them different from other groups of animals. They have fur or hair, their bodies are always at a fixed warm temperature, and their brains are better developed than those of animals in other groups. Nearly all mammals give birth to live young, rather than lay eggs, and all mammal mothers suckle their young with milk.

Mammals are very adaptable and different species live in almost every part of the world – from snowy mountains and scorching deserts to deep oceans.

There are only about 4,500 species of mammals in the world, compared with 700,000 insects. Just over 70 species of mammals live in Britain and Ireland.

Territory and hibernation

Two major threats to mammals' survival are predators (or enemies) and food shortage. Most mammals are protected from predators by their colour, which camouflages them, and by their sharp senses that warn them of danger before it is too late. The most vulnerable species (small rodents for example) breed very fast to make up for the numbers that are killed. Defending a territory and hibernation are two ways that mammals survive a food shortage.

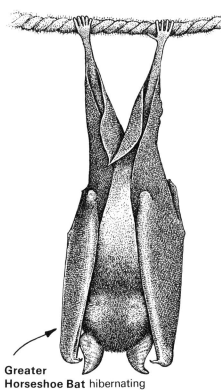

Greater Horseshoe Bat hibernating

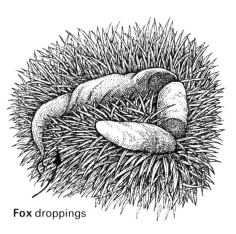

Fox droppings

Many mammals establish their own special feeding territory which they defend against intruders of the same species. Some mammals mark the boundaries with urine, droppings or scent from special glands.

To avoid the long winter, when food is scarce, some mammals hibernate, which means they go into a deep sleep. Before hibernation, they eat much more than usual. The extra fat keeps them going through the winter. When asleep, the heart beat and breathing rate slow down and the mammal's temperature drops. Its muscles become rigid so that it feels stiff and cold to the touch. Food reserves in the body are used up very slowly.

Feeding

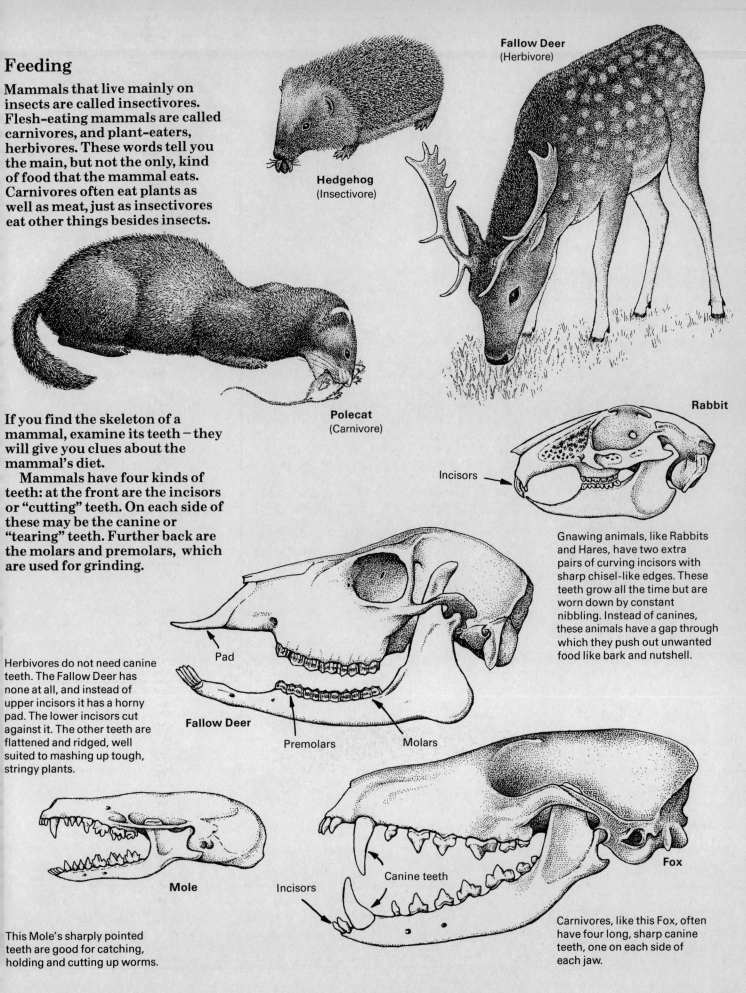

Mammals that live mainly on insects are called insectivores. Flesh-eating mammals are called carnivores, and plant-eaters, herbivores. These words tell you the main, but not the only, kind of food that the mammal eats. Carnivores often eat plants as well as meat, just as insectivores eat other things besides insects.

Hedgehog
(Insectivore)

Fallow Deer
(Herbivore)

Polecat
(Carnivore)

If you find the skeleton of a mammal, examine its teeth – they will give you clues about the mammal's diet.

Mammals have four kinds of teeth: at the front are the incisors or "cutting" teeth. On each side of these may be the canine or "tearing" teeth. Further back are the molars and premolars, which are used for grinding.

Rabbit

Incisors

Gnawing animals, like Rabbits and Hares, have two extra pairs of curving incisors with sharp chisel-like edges. These teeth grow all the time but are worn down by constant nibbling. Instead of canines, these animals have a gap through which they push out unwanted food like bark and nutshell.

Herbivores do not need canine teeth. The Fallow Deer has none at all, and instead of upper incisors it has a horny pad. The lower incisors cut against it. The other teeth are flattened and ridged, well suited to mashing up tough, stringy plants.

Pad

Fallow Deer

Premolars   Molars

Mole

Incisors

Canine teeth

Fox

This Mole's sharply pointed teeth are good for catching, holding and cutting up worms.

Carnivores, like this Fox, often have four long, sharp canine teeth, one on each side of each jaw.

Part 3 written by
Su Swallow

Consultant Editor
Alfred Leutscher, B.Sc., F.Z.S.

Part 3
PONDS & STREAMS

Many different kinds of animals and plants are attracted to fresh water. This section of the book shows the common species of birds, fishes, insects, mammals, plants and amphibians that live in and around fresh water in Europe. It tells you how to find them, and how they have adapted themselves to life near the water.

This section also explains how to make a collection of things like frogs, toads, and insects, so that you can study them at home. Remember to always put animals back when you have finished looking at them.

If you feel you would like to go further with your study of freshwater life, you could try contacting your local natural history society. You may find members who have a special interest in a local pond or stretch of river and who would be keen to explore with you.

How to Start

The best time to study streams and ponds is in the spring and summer, when the plants are flowering and the animals are most active. But winter is a very good time to spot birds.

Move slowly and quietly and be careful your shadow does not alarm the fishes. You will find more life near the bank, where there is more plant cover.

Look for freshwater life in lakes, rivers, ditches and canals. You may even find plants or insects in drinking troughs and rainwater tubs.

What to Take

Empty margarine pot for watching animals

Fishing net

Jars

Binoculars

Magnifying glass

REMEMBER!
NEVER GO INTO THE WATER IF YOU CAN'T SWIM. IT IS BEST TO GO WITH A FRIEND. DON'T WADE INTO RIVERS OR DEEP STREAMS. THERE MAY BE STRONG CURRENTS.

DO'S AND DON'TS

DO TEST WATER DEPTH WITH A LONG POLE BEFORE WADING IN.

DON'T USE LOGS OR STONES AS STEPPING-STONES WITHOUT TESTING THEM FIRST.

DO REPLACE STONES AND LOGS EXACTLY AS YOU FOUND THEM.

DO KEEP JARS WITH SPECIMENS IN THE SHADE TO KEEP THE WATER COOL.

DON'T HANDLE ANYTHING YOU CATCH. PUT IT STRAIGHT INTO A DISH OR JAR.

DON'T SMASH ICE ON PONDS IN WINTER. THIS WILL DISTURB ANIMALS LIVING THERE.

DON'T STAMP YOUR FEET OR MOVE QUICKLY. THIS WILL FRIGHTEN ANIMALS.

DON'T TAKE TOO MANY ANIMALS OR WHOLE PLANTS. PART OF A PLANT WILL BE ENOUGH TO IDENTIFY IT.

DO PUT ANIMALS AND PLANTS BACK INTO THE POND AS SOON AS POSSIBLE.

A Pond Survey

Ask some friends to help make a map of your pond, showing the plants and animals you find. If you look carefully, you might find something rare. Repeat the survey to see how pond life changes with the seasons. Check for signs of pollution. You can survey part of a stream in exactly the same way.

What to Look for

Even a small pond can support a surprising variety of life if it is not too shaded or polluted. Here are some of the animals to look for and their hiding places.

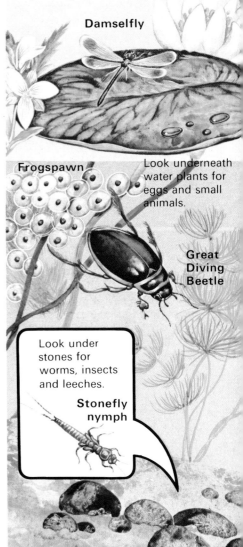

Damselfly

Frogspawn

Look underneath water plants for eggs and small animals.

Great Diving Beetle

Look under stones for worms, insects and leeches.

Stonefly nymph

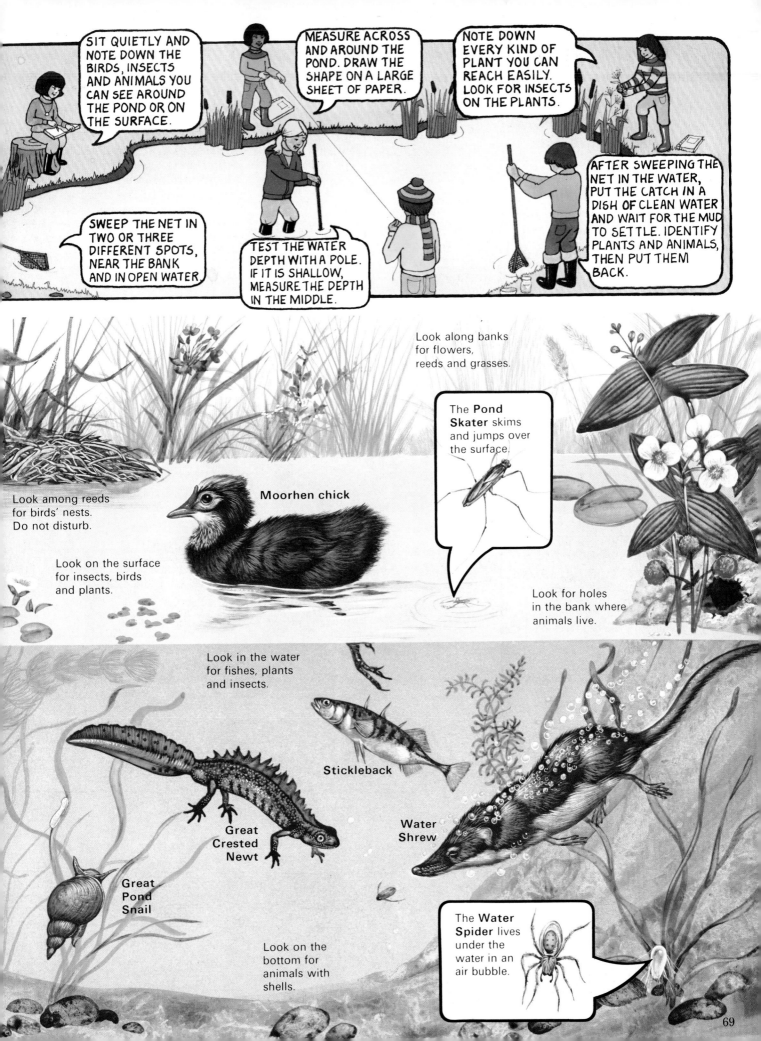

SIT QUIETLY AND NOTE DOWN THE BIRDS, INSECTS AND ANIMALS YOU CAN SEE AROUND THE POND OR ON THE SURFACE.

MEASURE ACROSS AND AROUND THE POND. DRAW THE SHAPE ON A LARGE SHEET OF PAPER.

NOTE DOWN EVERY KIND OF PLANT YOU CAN REACH EASILY. LOOK FOR INSECTS ON THE PLANTS.

AFTER SWEEPING THE NET IN THE WATER, PUT THE CATCH IN A DISH OF CLEAN WATER AND WAIT FOR THE MUD TO SETTLE. IDENTIFY PLANTS AND ANIMALS, THEN PUT THEM BACK.

SWEEP THE NET IN TWO OR THREE DIFFERENT SPOTS, NEAR THE BANK AND IN OPEN WATER.

TEST THE WATER DEPTH WITH A POLE. IF IT IS SHALLOW, MEASURE THE DEPTH IN THE MIDDLE.

Look along banks for flowers, reeds and grasses.

The **Pond Skater** skims and jumps over the surface.

Look among reeds for birds' nests. Do not disturb.

Moorhen chick

Look on the surface for insects, birds and plants.

Look for holes in the bank where animals live.

Look in the water for fishes, plants and insects.

Stickleback

Water Shrew

Great Crested Newt

Great Pond Snail

Look on the bottom for animals with shells.

The **Water Spider** lives under the water in an air bubble.

Living Together

In a thriving pond there is a balance of different kinds of animals and plants, so that there is enough food for them all to survive. It is important not to disturb this balance.

How Plants Help

Animals living in water need a gas called oxygen to breathe. They get some from the surface, but water plants also give off oxygen when they make their food. Plants need sunlight to make food and produce oxygen.

Canadian Pondweed

Try this experiment: put some Canadian Pondweed in water in the sun. Oxygen bubbles will soon appear.

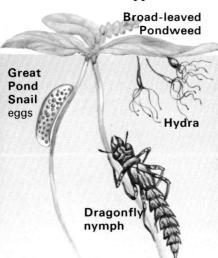

Broad-leaved Pondweed

Great Pond Snail eggs

Hydra

Dragonfly nymph

Plants not only produce oxygen for animals to breathe, but also help in other ways. They provide shade and shelter from enemies. They act as supports for eggs and tiny animals. Some insects use plant stems to climb out of the water when they are changing into winged adults.

Pond Food Chain

The process of one animal eating another and then being eaten by a larger animal is called a food chain. In the chain shown here, there are six links joined by arrows. At the top is the Heron which eats everything in the second link including Perch. Perch eat animals in the third link and so on down to the Algae at the bottom. Because each animal eats many things, a pond has many different food chains.

There are more animals at the bottom of the chain than at the top. This is because these animals are small, and a larger animal needs to eat many of them to survive.

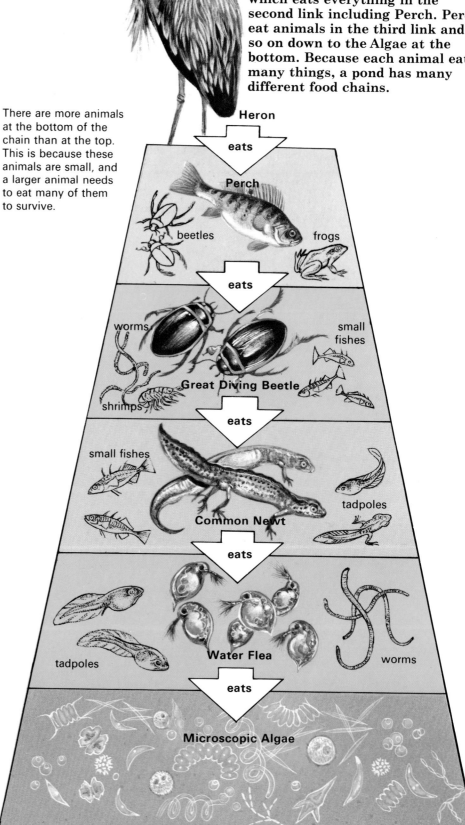

Heron

eats

Perch

beetles

frogs

eats

worms

small fishes

Great Diving Beetle

shrimps

eats

small fishes

Common Newt

tadpoles

eats

tadpoles

Water Flea

worms

eats

Microscopic Algae

Pollution

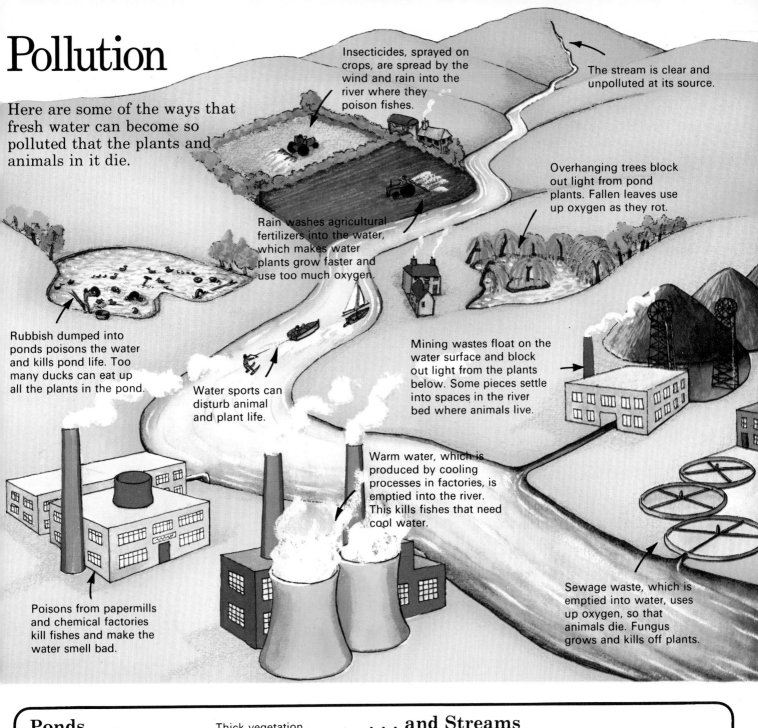

Here are some of the ways that fresh water can become so polluted that the plants and animals in it die.

Insecticides, sprayed on crops, are spread by the wind and rain into the river where they poison fishes.

The stream is clear and unpolluted at its source.

Overhanging trees block out light from pond plants. Fallen leaves use up oxygen as they rot.

Rain washes agricultural fertilizers into the water, which makes water plants grow faster and use too much oxygen.

Rubbish dumped into ponds poisons the water and kills pond life. Too many ducks can eat up all the plants in the pond.

Water sports can disturb animal and plant life.

Mining wastes float on the water surface and block out light from the plants below. Some pieces settle into spaces in the river bed where animals live.

Warm water, which is produced by cooling processes in factories, is emptied into the river. This kills fishes that need cool water.

Poisons from papermills and chemical factories kill fishes and make the water smell bad.

Sewage waste, which is emptied into water, uses up oxygen, so that animals die. Fungus grows and kills off plants.

Ponds . . .   . . . and Streams

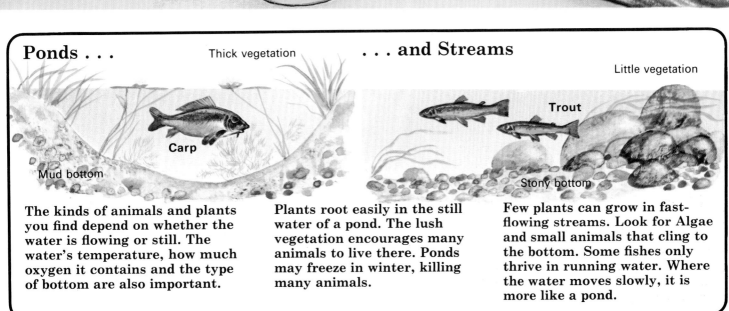

Thick vegetation

Little vegetation

Trout

Carp

Mud bottom

Stony bottom

The kinds of animals and plants you find depend on whether the water is flowing or still. The water's temperature, how much oxygen it contains and the type of bottom are also important.

Plants root easily in the still water of a pond. The lush vegetation encourages many animals to live there. Ponds may freeze in winter, killing many animals.

Few plants can grow in fast-flowing streams. Look for Algae and small animals that cling to the bottom. Some fishes only thrive in running water. Where the water moves slowly, it is more like a pond.

Plants of Ponds and Streams

Pond plants can be divided into groups depending on the zones, or areas, where they grow. Remember that the zones often overlap, and that you may not find all of the zones in one pond. Many of these common freshwater plants also grow in streams and rivers.

Notice how delicate many of the plants in deep water are. They do not need thick stems to support them, because the water holds them up. Their leaves are rather fine and thin because they do not need to hold water as land plants do.

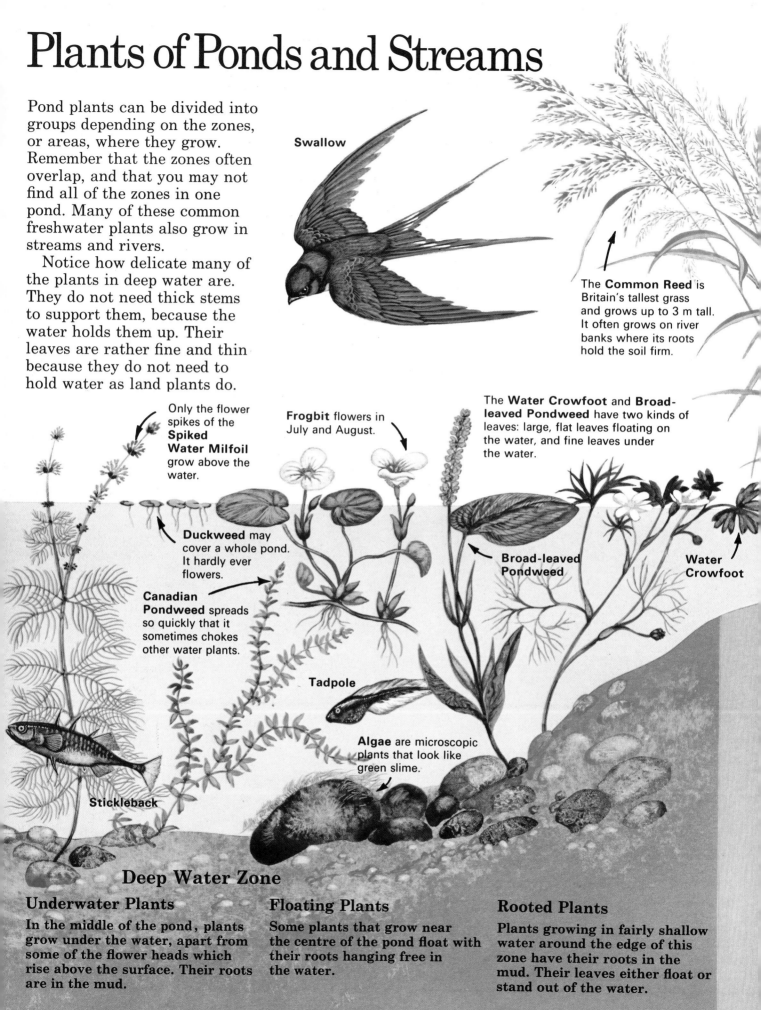

Swallow

The **Common Reed** is Britain's tallest grass and grows up to 3 m tall. It often grows on river banks where its roots hold the soil firm.

Only the flower spikes of the **Spiked Water Milfoil** grow above the water.

Frogbit flowers in July and August.

The **Water Crowfoot** and **Broad-leaved Pondweed** have two kinds of leaves: large, flat leaves floating on the water, and fine leaves under the water.

Duckweed may cover a whole pond. It hardly ever flowers.

Canadian Pondweed spreads so quickly that it sometimes chokes other water plants.

Broad-leaved Pondweed

Water Crowfoot

Tadpole

Algae are microscopic plants that look like green slime.

Stickleback

Deep Water Zone

Underwater Plants

In the middle of the pond, plants grow under the water, apart from some of the flower heads which rise above the surface. Their roots are in the mud.

Floating Plants

Some plants that grow near the centre of the pond float with their roots hanging free in the water.

Rooted Plants

Plants growing in fairly shallow water around the edge of this zone have their roots in the mud. Their leaves either float or stand out of the water.

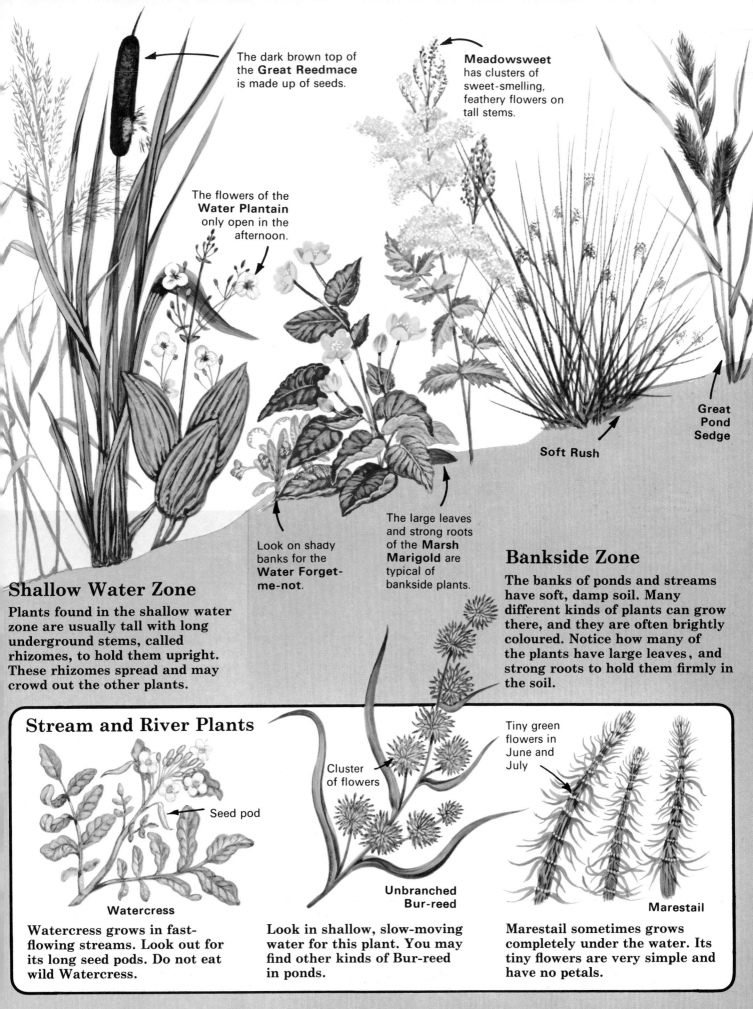

The dark brown top of the **Great Reedmace** is made up of seeds.

Meadowsweet has clusters of sweet-smelling, feathery flowers on tall stems.

The flowers of the **Water Plantain** only open in the afternoon.

Look on shady banks for the **Water Forget-me-not**.

The large leaves and strong roots of the **Marsh Marigold** are typical of bankside plants.

Soft Rush

Great Pond Sedge

Shallow Water Zone

Plants found in the shallow water zone are usually tall with long underground stems, called rhizomes, to hold them upright. These rhizomes spread and may crowd out the other plants.

Bankside Zone

The banks of ponds and streams have soft, damp soil. Many different kinds of plants can grow there, and they are often brightly coloured. Notice how many of the plants have large leaves, and strong roots to hold them firmly in the soil.

Stream and River Plants

Seed pod

Cluster of flowers

Tiny green flowers in June and July

Watercress

Unbranched Bur-reed

Marestail

Watercress grows in fast-flowing streams. Look out for its long seed pods. Do not eat wild Watercress.

Look in shallow, slow-moving water for this plant. You may find other kinds of Bur-reed in ponds.

Marestail sometimes grows completely under the water. Its tiny flowers are very simple and have no petals.

How Water Plants Grow

Many water plants grow from seeds. The seeds are formed after pollen from the male part of the flower (the stamen) reaches the female part (the style) of the same kind of flower. When the seeds are ripe, they are scattered and some of them grow. Some water plants can also spread by growing new plants from their rhizomes, or underground stems.

Some underwater plants do not spread by seed. Instead, new plants may grow from winter buds or from pieces that break off the old plant.

1 How Pollen Spreads

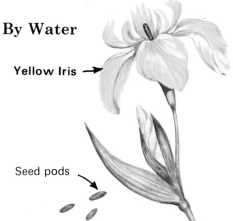

Purple Loosestrife

Water Mint

Pollen from some plants is spread by insects. The bright colours and scent attract insects, and the pollen rubs off on to their bodies. Then they carry it to other plants.

2

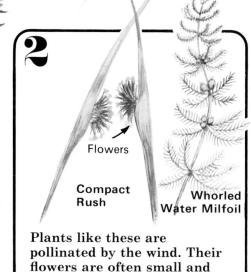

Flowers

Compact Rush

Whorled Water Milfoil

Plants like these are pollinated by the wind. Their flowers are often small and dull, because they do not need to attract insects.

How Seeds are Scattered

By Wind

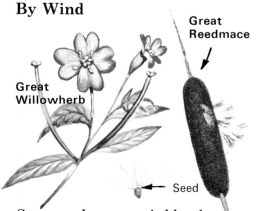

Great Reedmace

Great Willowherb

Seed

Some seeds are carried by the wind on a hairy parachute. Willowherb seeds may travel as far away as 150 kilometres.

By Water

Yellow Iris →

Seed pods

Some plant seeds, like these pods from a Yellow Iris, are carried by water. They open when softened by water.

By Animals

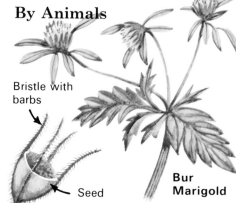

Bristle with barbs

Seed

Bur Marigold

Seeds with barbs, or hooks, catch on to animals' fur or people's clothing and later drop off.

How Water Lilies Grow

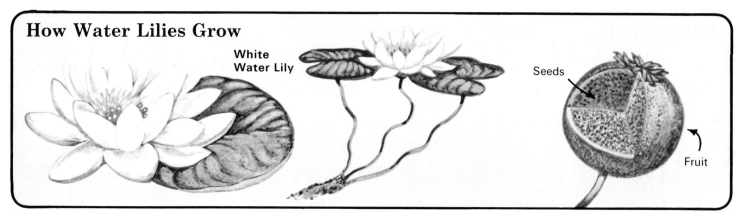

White Water Lily

Seeds

Fruit

Look in ponds for the White Water Lily. Its leaves and flowers float on the surface, but at night the flowers close, and sometimes sink just below the surface until morning.

The Water Lily is anchored to the bottom by stout rhizomes. The leaf stalks grow up from these stems at an angle. If the water level rises, they straighten up so that the leaves can still float.

The flowers are pollinated by insects. When the fruits are ripe, they sink to the bottom and release up to 2,000 seeds. The seeds float away, and some sink and start to grow into new plants.

3

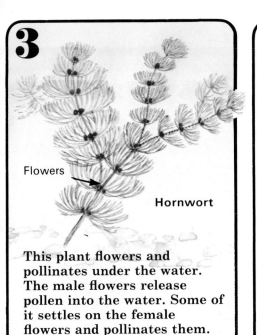

Flowers

Hornwort

This plant flowers and pollinates under the water. The male flowers release pollen into the water. Some of it settles on the female flowers and pollinates them.

How Other Water Plants Spread

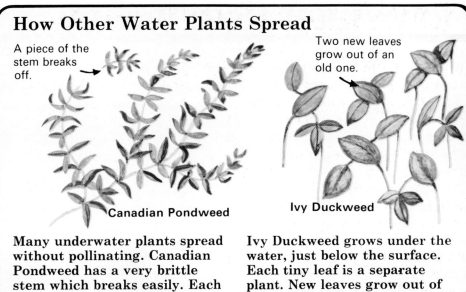

A piece of the stem breaks off.

Two new leaves grow out of an old one.

Canadian Pondweed

Ivy Duckweed

Many underwater plants spread without pollinating. Canadian Pondweed has a very brittle stem which breaks easily. Each piece that breaks off grows into a new plant.

Ivy Duckweed grows under the water, just below the surface. Each tiny leaf is a separate plant. New leaves grow out of slits in the sides of old ones and then break away to become new plants.

By Explosion

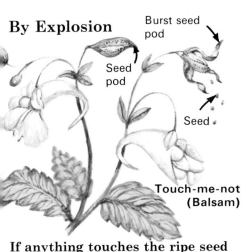

Burst seed pod

Seed pod

Seed

Touch-me-not (Balsam)

If anything touches the ripe seed pods of this plant, they burst open and the seeds fall out.

Watching a Plant Grow

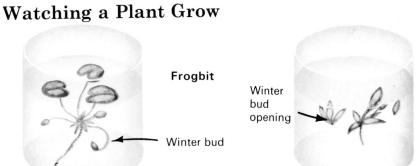

Frogbit

Winter bud opening

Winter bud

Frogbit grows winter buds on underwater roots. Each bud contains a new plant and a store of food. When the buds are ripe, they break off and sink. In spring, when the stored food is

used up, the buds float to the surface and grow into new plants. Collect some Frogbit in the autumn, and watch how it grows. Keep it cool in a jar of pond water.

In Winter

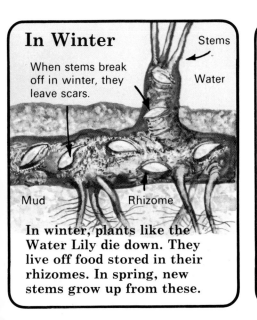

Stems

When stems break off in winter, they leave scars.

Water

Mud

Rhizome

In winter, plants like the Water Lily die down. They live off food stored in their rhizomes. In spring, new stems grow up from these.

Insect-Eating Plants

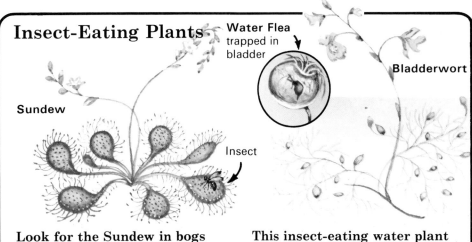

Water Flea trapped in bladder

Bladderwort

Sundew

Insect

Look for the Sundew in bogs and marshes. It traps insects on its hairs and digests them with special juices.

This insect-eating water plant catches tiny animals in its air-filled, underwater bladders. Then it feeds on them.

Watching Water Birds

Birdwatching by ponds and streams is exciting because of the variety of birds you may find there. Some birds spend most of their lives by water. Others may come to drink and bathe. In winter, sea birds fly inland for food and shelter.

The best place to look for birds is by water surrounded by thick vegetation. Early morning is a good time to see them.

In parks, some water birds are tame enough to be fed. Others are shy, so you must hide and wait quietly to see them. Keep a record of the birds you spot and their habits. If you find a nest, be sure not to disturb it.

Feeding

Watch the birds on and around a pond closely. See how many ways of feeding you can spot, the different bill shapes and how they are suited to these feeding methods. Time how long diving ducks stay under the water.

Mallards are dabbling ducks. They feed near the surface and eat mostly plants. They also up-end to get food from deep water.

Tufted Ducks dive down one or two metres for water plants, insects and small fishes.

Female   Male

Wigeon feed mainly on grasses and grain, cropped from fields. They also dabble in water.

The **Swift** feeds and even sleeps on the wing. It eats flies and beetles.

The **Shoveler** uses its wide bill to sieve food from water and mud.

The **Bittern** nests in reed beds where it is camouflaged well. It eats frogs, small fishes and insects.

The **Teal** is Britain's smallest duck. It is a surface-feeder and eats mainly water plants and their seeds.

The **Moorhen** eats plants and small animals in the water as well as seeds and grain on land.

The **Kingfisher** dives for small fishes and insects. It sometimes beats a fish against a branch to kill it. Then it swallows the fish head first, so that the fins and scales do not open and choke the bird.

Flocks in Flight

1 Taking a Count

To work out the number of birds in a flock, count the first ten birds. Then guess what part that is of the whole flock. Multiply to get the total number of birds.

2 Flight Patterns

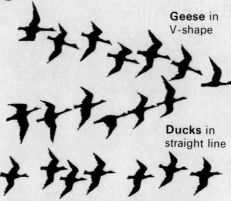

Geese in V-shape

Ducks in straight line

The pattern a flock forms can help you to identify the birds. Many birds fly in a line or a V-shape.

3 Keeping Together

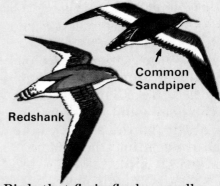

Common Sandpiper

Redshank

Birds that fly in flocks usually have distinctive markings for others to follow. They also call to each other to keep together, especially after dark.

The **Greylag Goose** spends a lot of time on land. It crops the grass with its bill.

Looking after Feathers

1 Bathing

Goosander

Water birds often bathe to keep clean. They flap their wings on the water and roll over to wet their bodies thoroughly. Then they shake themselves dry.

2 Oiling

Great Crested Grebe

Preen gland

Next, water birds spread oil from the preen glands near their tails, by rubbing their bills and heads over their feathers. The oil is good for the condition of the feathers.

3 Preening

Pintail

Finally, they fluff up their feathers, nibble each one and draw them through their bills. This cleans and oils them still more, and settles them back into place.

How Feathers Work

Duck feather

Shaft

Barb

The barbs on a bird's feather grow out of the shaft. They fit together very closely, rather like the teeth of a zip. This helps keep the bird's body dry and warm.

Birds: Mating and Nesting

Birds become very active in the spring when most of them breed. The male birds attract females by showing off their bright feathers. Some develop crests and ruffs of feathers at this time. They make special mating calls and perform acrobatics in the air or on the water. Sometimes both male and female birds take part in these courtship displays.

When the female has accepted the male, a nest is built. Notice what materials each kind of bird collects for its nest.

Courtship

Great Crested Grebes

Male

Female

Great Crested Grebes start their courtship early in the year. Head-shaking (above) is a common display. The birds swim towards each other, calling and shaking their heads from side to side.

After head-shaking, the Grebes may "dance" together. First they dive to collect weed. Then they swim towards one another and rise out of the water, swaying their bills and paddling hard.

Fighting

Mute Swan

Greylag Goose

Coots

This Swan is puffing out its feathers to frighten away an enemy. Sometimes birds fight to defend their nest or territory.

This Greylag Goose is standing in a threat position to chase away other adult geese that might come too close to its nest or territory.

Coots fight with their claws, holding themselves up with their wings. Fights do not last very long, and usually only the males take part.

Nesting

Reed Warblers

Sand Martins

Dippers

The Reed Warbler nests in reed beds. The grass nest is shaped like a deep basket, so that the eggs and young birds cannot fall out, even in a strong wind.

Look for groups of Sand Martins nesting in mud or sand banks. Each nest is at the end of a tunnel, which the birds dig with their feet and bills.

The Dipper hides its nest in cracks between rocks near a stream. It also nests under bridges or behind waterfalls. The cup-shaped nest is made of moss and grasses.

Kingfishers

Female

Male

Male

Female

Pochards

Mallards

Male

Female

Some male birds, like the Kingfisher, make a present of food to the female during courtship. When she has accepted it, they are ready to mate.

The Mallard is a common duck, and you are quite likely to see the male's striking courtship display. He dives, flaps his wings, sprays water with his bill, whistles and grunts. The female draws his attention by jerking her head to and fro.

To impress a female, the male Pochard swims around her, jerking his head backwards and forwards.

Looking after the Young

Grey Herons

Some birds, like the Heron, are born helpless. They are blind, featherless, and cannot leave the nest for over a month. Young Herons beg for food by pecking at their parents' bills. Other young birds beg with loud cries or gaping beaks. However, some chicks, like Ducks and Grebes, can swim a few hours after hatching. Ducklings can also feed themselves.

Keeping the Young Safe

Little Grebes (or Dabchicks)

Little Grebes can swim soon after they hatch, but sometimes they climb on to their parents' backs to keep safe from danger.

Little Ringed Plover

Like many other birds that nest on the ground, the Little Ringed Plover may pretend to be hurt to draw an enemy away from its nest.

How Insects Grow

You can find some strange and exciting insects in ponds and streams, even in polluted water. Most insects go through several stages of development between the egg and the adult. (Follow the steps in the development of the Caddis Fly.) The early stages may last for years, but the adult may live only for a few hours or days.

Some water insects, like water beetles, spend all their lives in the water, while others, like the Alder Fly, leave the water when fully grown.

The Caddis Fly

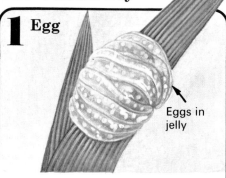

1 Egg

Eggs in jelly

Caddis Flies develop in fresh water. The eggs are laid in jelly on plants or stones, either above or in the water.

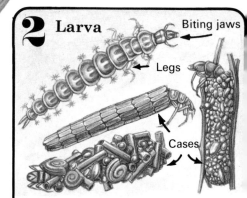

2 Larva

Biting jaws

Legs

Cases

When the larva hatches from the egg, it makes itself a protective case of shells, stones or leaves. It eats plants on the pond bottom.

Where Insects Lay Eggs

1 On the Water

Cocoon

Mast

The Great Silver Beetle lays its eggs in a silky cocoon on the water's surface. The hollow "mast" is to allow air to reach the eggs.

2 Above the Water

Cluster of **Alder Fly** eggs

Adult **Alder Fly**

Look for insect eggs on water plants and stones above the water. When the larvae hatch, they fall or crawl down into the water.

3 Below the Water

Single **Water Scorpion** egg

Breathing tubes

Some insects lay their eggs under the water, on plants or stones, or on the mud bottom. The Water Scorpion lays its eggs on plant stems.

Larvae and Nymphs

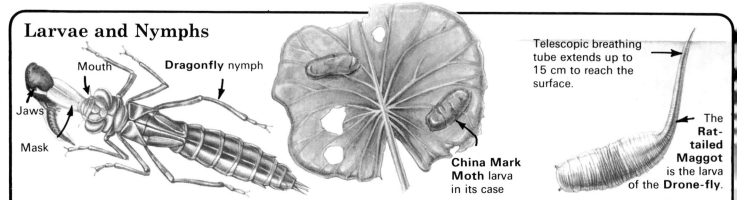

Mouth

Dragonfly nymph

Jaws

Mask

A young Dragonfly, when it hatches from the egg, is called a nymph. It has a strong pair of jaws fixed to a hinge, called a mask. The mask shoots out to catch prey.

China Mark Moth larva in its case

Look for small holes in the leaves of Water Lilies and Pondweed. Underneath, you may see this moth larva, which makes a case out of the leaves and also feeds on them.

Telescopic breathing tube extends up to 15 cm to reach the surface.

The **Rat-tailed Maggot** is the larva of the **Drone-fly**.

Look in mud for the Rat-tailed Maggot. Scoop up some mud and a little water in a dish, and wait for it to settle. Look for the Maggot's breathing tube.

3 Pupa

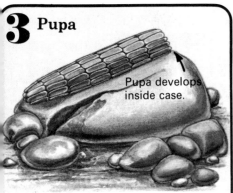

Pupa develops inside case.

After about a year, the larva stops eating and changes into a pupa inside the case. During the winter, the pupa slowly develops into an adult Caddis Fly inside the case.

4 Adult

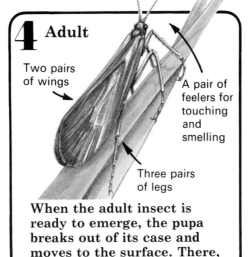

Two pairs of wings

A pair of feelers for touching and smelling

Three pairs of legs

When the adult insect is ready to emerge, the pupa breaks out of its case and moves to the surface. There, the adult splits out of its pupal skin and flies away.

An Underwater Viewer

Place sealed end in water.

Use a large tin to make this underwater viewer. Remove the top and bottom with a tin opener. Cover one end with clear plastic wrap and attach it tightly with a rubber band. Look through the open end.

A Dragonfly Emerges

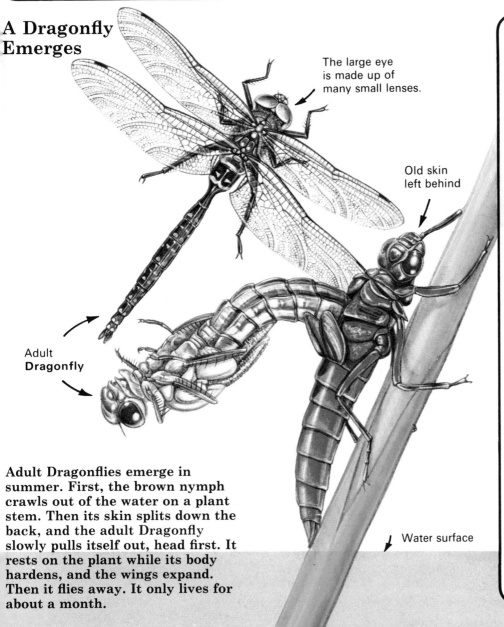

The large eye is made up of many small lenses.

Old skin left behind

Adult **Dragonfly**

Water surface

Adult Dragonflies emerge in summer. First, the brown nymph crawls out of the water on a plant stem. Then its skin splits down the back, and the adult Dragonfly slowly pulls itself out, head first. It rests on the plant while its body hardens, and the wings expand. Then it flies away. It only lives for about a month.

Watching Gnats Grow

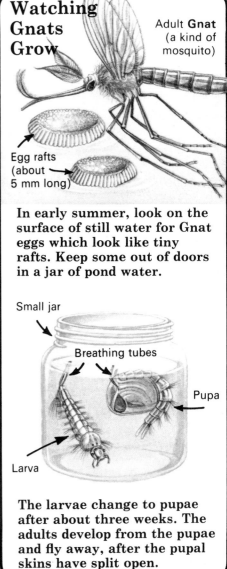

Adult **Gnat** (a kind of mosquito)

Egg rafts (about 5 mm long)

In early summer, look on the surface of still water for Gnat eggs which look like tiny rafts. Keep some out of doors in a jar of pond water.

Small jar

Breathing tubes

Pupa

Larva

The larvae change to pupae after about three weeks. The adults develop from the pupae and fly away, after the pupal skins have split open.

Watching Insects

If you sit by a pond or stream, you will soon spot several kinds of insects. Look in the air, on the water's surface and in the water. To help you to identify an insect, make a note of its colour, the shape and number of its wings, where you saw it and other details.

Remember that all adult insects have bodies with three parts, three pairs of legs, and usually a pair of antennae or feelers. Many have wings at some time in their lives.

Above the Water

A **Damselfly** at rest holds its wings together.

Swarms of **Mayflies** rise and fall over the water.

A **Mayfly** has two or three long threads at the end of its body.

Dragonflies fly in pairs when mating.

Look for these flying insects in spring and early summer, when they emerge from the pupa or nymph. Most stay close to the water, and they all breed there.

How Insects Stay on the Surface

Use blotting paper to place the needle on the water.

The paper will sink, but the needle will stay afloat.

A thin film on the surface of the water holds insects up. See how this works by floating a needle on water.

On the Surface

The **Water Measurer** moves slowly. The hairs on its body stop it from getting wet.

The **Pond Skater** slides rapidly over the surface. It can also jump.

Tiny **Springtails** can jump 30 cm using their hinged tails.

Whirligig Beetles whirl and spin, without colliding, while looking for food.

Notice the different ways that these insects move on the water surface. They feed mostly on dead insects that fall on the water.

Under the Water

The **Water Boatman** swims and takes in air at the surface, upside down.

It has strong legs for swimming.

Breathing tube

Its antenna breaks the surface film while it collects air.

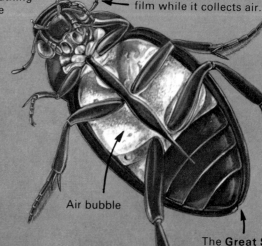

Air bubble

Most insects breathe by taking in air through holes in their bodies. Many underwater insects carry a bubble of air on their bodies, which they collect at the surface and replace when it is used up.

The **Water Scorpion** takes in air at the surface through a breathing tube. It stores air under its wing cases.

The **Great Silver Beetle** carries a bubble of air trapped by the hairs on its underside.

82

How Insects Feed

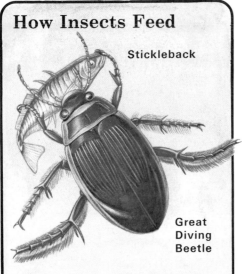

Sticklebick

Great Diving Beetle

Many water beetles eat other animals. The Great Diving Beetle feeds on tadpoles and fishes. Its prey is often larger than itself.

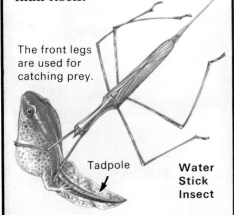

The front legs are used for catching prey.

Tadpole

Water Stick Insect

This insect hides among reed stems, waiting for its prey. It shoots out its front legs to catch any passing animal and then sucks out the juices.

Lesser Water Boatman

The Lesser Water Boatman feeds on algae and rotting plants on the bottom. Unlike the Water Boatman, it swims right side up.

Making an Insect Aquarium

This picture shows the things you will need to make an aquarium. You can buy some of them at pet shops. Keep the aquarium near a window, but not in direct sunlight. If you use tap water, add some pond water and leave it for a few days before adding the animals.

Nymphs and Larvae

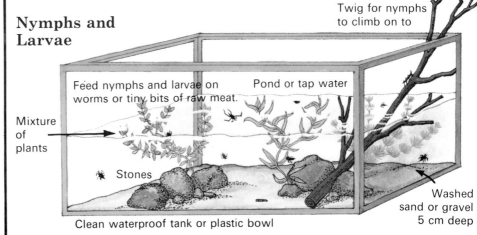

Twig for nymphs to climb on to

Feed nymphs and larvae on worms or tiny bits of raw meat.

Pond or tap water

Mixture of plants

Stones

Washed sand or gravel 5 cm deep

Clean waterproof tank or plastic bowl

Flying Insects

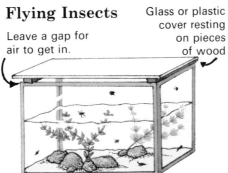

Glass or plastic cover resting on pieces of wood

Leave a gap for air to get in.

Feed beetles on worms or tiny bits of raw meat.

To keep water insects that can fly, like beetles, put a lid or netting on the aquarium to stop them from escaping.

Tiny Insects

Lid with air holes

Margarine pot

Magnifying glass

You can make a collection of tiny insects very easily. Put them in a jar or pot, with some pond water, a little mud and a few plants.

Fierce Insects

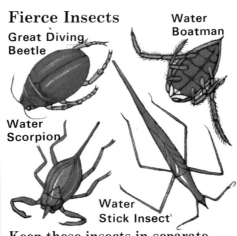

Great Diving Beetle

Water Boatman

Water Scorpion

Water Stick Insect

Keep these insects in separate containers, or they will eat each other. Feed them on pieces of meat or worms.

REMEMBER! ONLY TAKE A FEW INSECTS FROM THE WATER. MAKE SURE THEY HAVE THE RIGHT FOOD AND ENOUGH ROOM. ALWAYS RETURN THEM TO THE POND OR STREAM WHEN YOU HAVE FINISHED STUDYING THEM.

Mammals

Most mammals that live near fresh water are very shy and are not often seen. Some are nocturnal, which means that they are only active at night. Often all you will hear is a "plop" as the animal leaps into the water to get away. Mammals can hear well and have a good sense of smell. So if you go animal tracking, approach the water quietly, facing the wind. You may find animal tracks or feeding signs. Try to identify them, so that you know which animal you are looking for!

Spot the Difference

Water Vole — Tiny ears — Short, furry tail

Brown Rat — Large ears — Blunt snout — Pointed snout — Long, naked tail

The Water Vole is often confused with the Brown Rat. They look rather alike and both are often seen swimming. Look at the differences carefully, so that you can tell them apart if you spot them. The Water Vole often swims under the water, but the Brown Rat keeps more to the surface of the water.

The **Harvest Mouse**, driven out of the cornfields by farm machinery, now often nests in reed beds. It is an expert climber and can hang by its tail. It comes out in the day.

This bat often flies over water in the daytime, hunting for insects. It can swim well too.

Daubenton's Bat

The **Brown Rat** prefers rivers and canals. Look for it at any time of day. It eats almost anything.

The **Water Shrew** sometimes leaps out of the water to catch insects. It also eats fishes and frogs. You may see it walking on the bottom of streams, looking for food.

Look on banks of large ponds and slow rivers for the Water Vole. You may see it dive into the water. After a swim, it grooms its fur.

Look for plant stems which have been bitten off. This could be the feeding spot of a Water Vole.

Holes in the bank, either above or below water, could be the entrance to a **Shrew's** or **Vole's** burrow.

Rare Mammals

Beaver

European Mink

Muskrat

The Muskrat is a large vole that lives in parts of Europe, but not in Britain. It swims fast and keeps near the surface of shallow, overgrown water.

A few Beavers survive in Europe, mostly in remote northern areas. They build their homes, called lodges, with branches or logs that they cut from trees.

Some Minks are wild, while others have escaped from fur farms. You might see one in a reed bed or by a river. They hunt and swim at night. They are very fierce.

The Otter

When it dives for fish, it shuts its ears and nostrils.

Waterproof fur

Spraints

Webbed toes for swimming

Its thick tail acts as a rudder.

The Otter is a shy, nocturnal animal. It lives in lonely places, and is well adapted for life in the water. It eats fishes, frogs and shellfish. Otter cubs are

born in a holt, a tunnel in the bank or among tree roots. Even the adults are playful and make slides down the river bank in the snow or mud. You might see

one of these slides, or find Otter droppings, called spraints, on a rock or clump of grass. Otters often leave behind remains of fish they have eaten.

Tracks

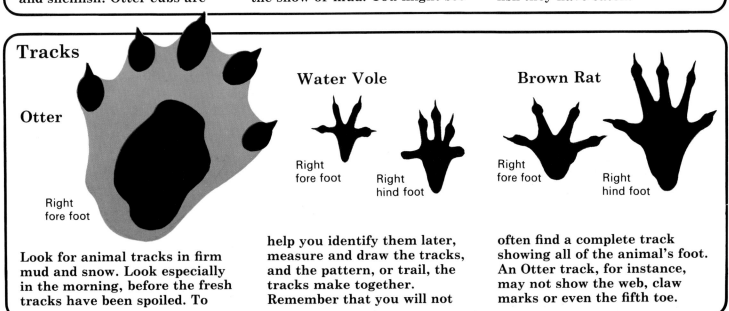

Otter

Right fore foot

Water Vole

Right fore foot

Right hind foot

Brown Rat

Right fore foot

Right hind foot

Look for animal tracks in firm mud and snow. Look especially in the morning, before the fresh tracks have been spoiled. To

help you identify them later, measure and draw the tracks, and the pattern, or trail, the tracks make together. Remember that you will not

often find a complete track showing all of the animal's foot. An Otter track, for instance, may not show the web, claw marks or even the fifth toe.

Fishes

There are nearly 40 kinds of freshwater fishes in Britain.

Notice which kinds prefer still or moving water, and make a check-list to help you to identify the fish: what colour and shape is it? Does it have whiskers, or barbels, near its mouth? Is it near the surface or on the bottom? How fast does it swim?

Most freshwater fishes spawn, or lay their eggs, in shallow water. Look for eggs among water plants and on the stones and sand of the bottom. Small fishes are called fry.

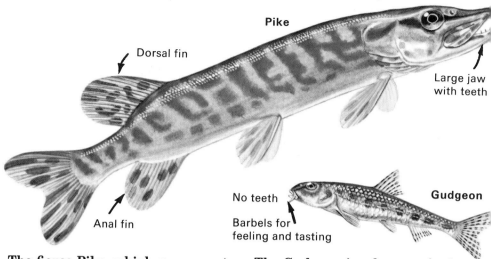

Pike

Dorsal fin

Large jaw with teeth

Anal fin

No teeth

Gudgeon

Barbels for feeling and tasting

The fierce Pike, which grows up to 1m long, hunts frogs, young birds, fishes, and even other Pike. It lurks in reeds, waiting for its prey, and then attacks with its sharp teeth.

The Gudgeon is a bottom-feeder. It sucks insect larvae, worms and shellfish into its mouth. Its mouth is toothless, but it has teeth in its throat which break up the food it swallows.

In a Pond

Most pond fishes are rounder and fatter than the slim, streamlined fishes of running water. They swim more slowly too.

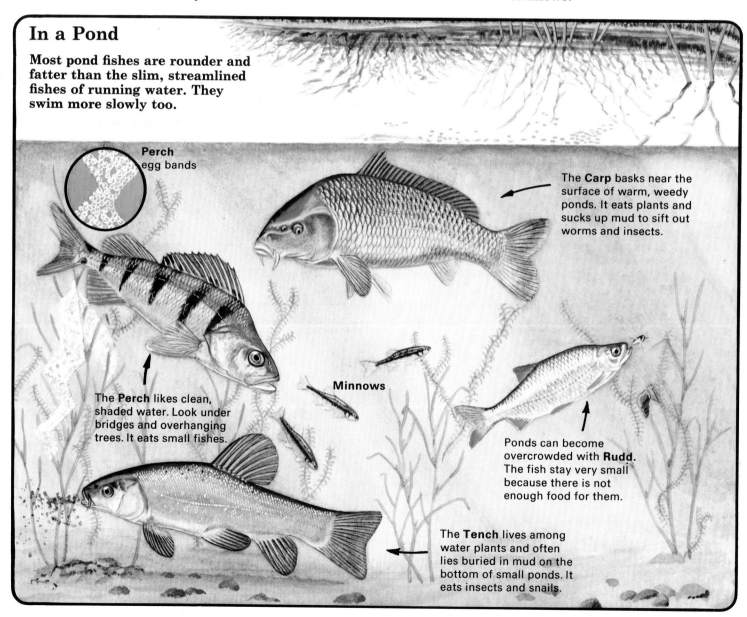

Perch egg bands

The **Carp** basks near the surface of warm, weedy ponds. It eats plants and sucks up mud to sift out worms and insects.

The **Perch** likes clean, shaded water. Look under bridges and overhanging trees. It eats small fishes.

Minnows

Ponds can become overcrowded with **Rudd**. The fish stay very small because there is not enough food for them.

The **Tench** lives among water plants and often lies buried in mud on the bottom of small ponds. It eats insects and snails.

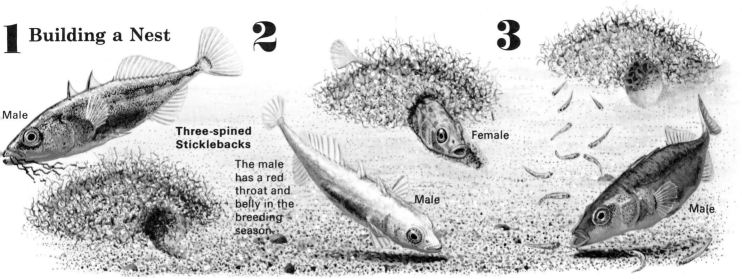

1 Building a Nest

Male

2

Three-spined Sticklebacks

The male has a red throat and belly in the breeding season.

Female

Male

3

Male

Look for this Stickleback in ponds and ditches. In May, a male builds a nest where the female will lay her eggs. He glues bits of plants together with sticky threads from

his body. The male "dances" to attract a female to the nest. The female leaves after laying the eggs. The male then fans the eggs with his fins to keep fresh water

flowing over them. When the eggs hatch, the male guards the fry. He chases away enemies and catches stray fry in his mouth to bring them back to the nest.

In a Stream

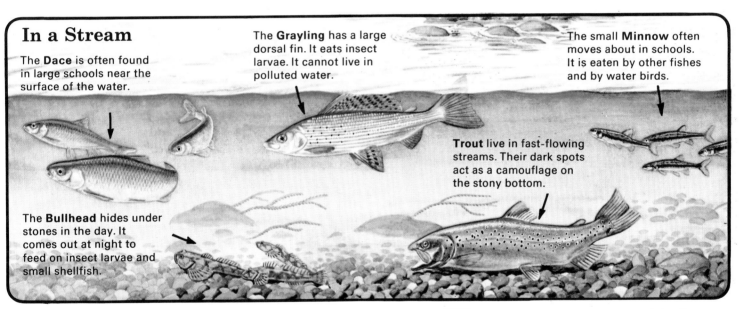

The **Dace** is often found in large schools near the surface of the water.

The **Grayling** has a large dorsal fin. It eats insect larvae. It cannot live in polluted water.

The small **Minnow** often moves about in schools. It is eaten by other fishes and by water birds.

Trout live in fast-flowing streams. Their dark spots act as a camouflage on the stony bottom.

The **Bullhead** hides under stones in the day. It comes out at night to feed on insect larvae and small shellfish.

Eels

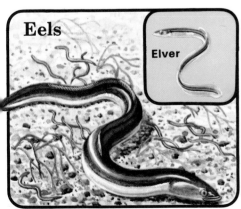

Elver

Eels live in fresh water until they are about ten years old. Then they move down rivers to the sea to breed and die. The young eels, called elvers, travel back to fresh water.

Salmon

Salmon spend some of their lives in the sea, but return to fresh water to breed. Most Salmon even reach the river where they were born. The female lays up to 15,000 eggs on the river bottom.

REMEMBER! IF YOU WANT TO SEE FISHES, APPROACH THE WATER SLOWLY AND QUIETLY. KEEP YOUR SHADOW OFF THE WATER. TRY FEEDING FISHES WITH BREAD OR MAGGOTS.

Frogs, Toads and Newts

Frogs, toads and newts are born in water, but spend most of their adult life on land. These animals are called amphibians. The young tadpoles develop from eggs, called spawn, laid in the water. They breathe by taking in oxygen from the water through their gills. As they grow, their gills and tails slowly disappear, and lungs and legs take their place (although newts keep their tails). Now the young amphibian leaves the water except when it returns to the pond to breed in spring.

Frogs

Common Frog

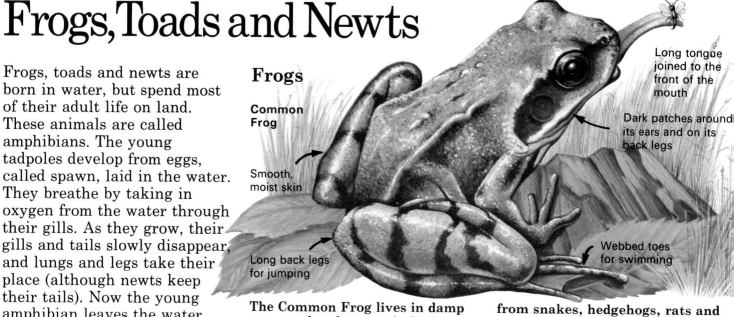

Smooth, moist skin

Long back legs for jumping

Long tongue joined to the front of the mouth

Dark patches around its ears and on its back legs

Webbed toes for swimming

The Common Frog lives in damp grass and undergrowth. Its basic colour can change to match its surroundings. This helps it to hide from snakes, hedgehogs, rats and other enemies. In winter, the frog hibernates in the mud bottom of a ditch or pond.

How Frogs Breed

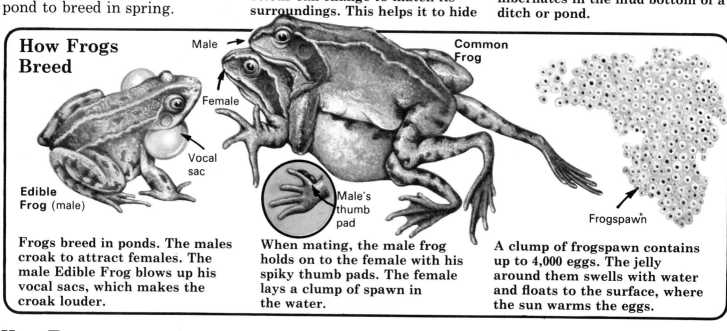

Male

Female

Vocal sac

Edible Frog (male)

Male's thumb pad

Common Frog

Frogspawn

Frogs breed in ponds. The males croak to attract females. The male Edible Frog blows up his vocal sacs, which makes the croak louder.

When mating, the male frog holds on to the female with his spiky thumb pads. The female lays a clump of spawn in the water.

A clump of frogspawn contains up to 4,000 eggs. The jelly around them swells with water and floats to the surface, where the sun warms the eggs.

How Frogspawn Develops

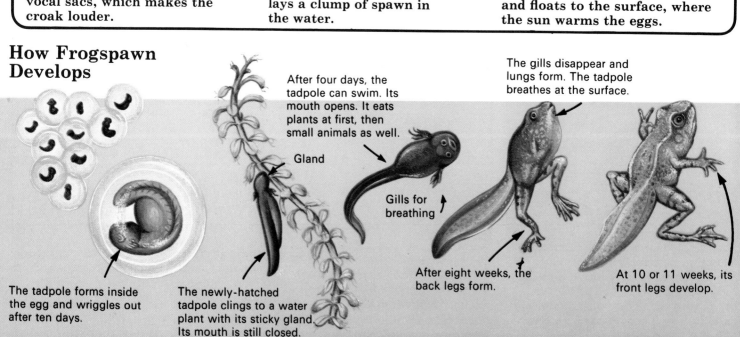

After four days, the tadpole can swim. Its mouth opens. It eats plants at first, then small animals as well.

Gland

The gills disappear and lungs form. The tadpole breathes at the surface.

Gills for breathing

The tadpole forms inside the egg and wriggles out after ten days.

The newly-hatched tadpole clings to a water plant with its sticky gland. Its mouth is still closed.

After eight weeks, the back legs form.

At 10 or 11 weeks, its front legs develop.

Toads

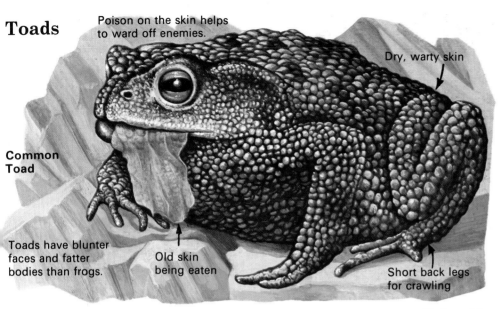

Poison on the skin helps to ward off enemies.

Dry, warty skin

Common Toad

Toads have blunter faces and fatter bodies than frogs.

Old skin being eaten

Short back legs for crawling

In the day, the Common Toad hides in holes in the ground. It hunts for food at night. A toad grows a new skin several times in the summer. It scrapes off the old one and eats it. In winter, it hibernates in an old animal burrow.

Danger

Toad

Grass Snake

If a toad is threatened by a Grass Snake, it may blow itself up so that the snake cannot swallow it.

Toadspawn

In spring, toads may travel for ten days to reach their breeding ponds. They mate like frogs, but lay eggs in ribbons about 2 m long.

At 12 or 13 weeks, the tail disappears and the tiny frog, 1 cm long, is ready to leave the water. It will be fully grown in three years. Few tadpoles survive to this stage. Most are eaten by other pond creatures.

Newts

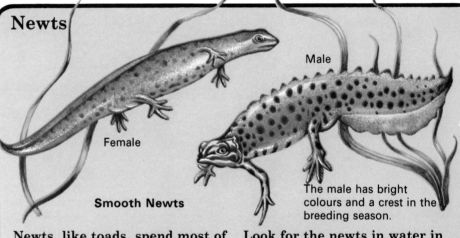

Male

Female

Smooth Newts

The male has bright colours and a crest in the breeding season.

Newts, like toads, spend most of their life on land, hiding by day and feeding at night. They look rather like lizards, but are not scaly.

Look for the newts in water in spring. You might see the male Smooth Newt's courtship dance. He arches his back and flicks his tail.

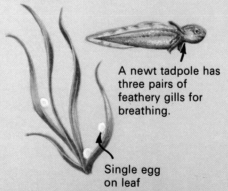

A newt tadpole has three pairs of feathery gills for breathing.

Single egg on leaf

Its front legs grow first. The tadpole eats water fleas and tiny worms.

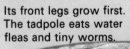

Its gills disappear and its lungs and back legs develop.

Newts lay their eggs singly, on water plants. The leaves are often bent over to protect the eggs. The tadpoles hatch after about two weeks. The young newts, or efts, are ready to leave the water in August, but some stay in the water until the next year.

Keeping Amphibians

Frogspawn

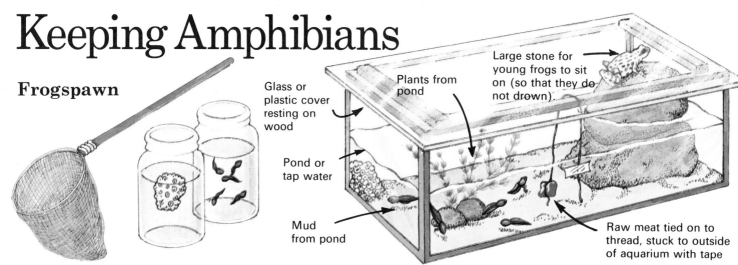

Glass or plastic cover resting on wood

Plants from pond

Large stone for young frogs to sit on (so that they do not drown).

Pond or tap water

Mud from pond

Raw meat tied on to thread, stuck to outside of aquarium with tape

How to collect: Look in ponds in March and April. Use a net to collect frogspawn. Put a little in a jar and return the rest to the water. If the eggs have already hatched, collect some tadpoles to study instead.

Where to keep: Put the aquarium in a light place, but out of direct sunlight. Change the water as soon as it smells bad. When the frogs have grown, return them to the edge of the pond where you found the spawn.

Feeding: Newly-hatched tadpoles will eat plants in the aquarium. After about a week, they will need raw meat too. Hang small pieces in the water, tied with thread, and replace them every two days.

Toads

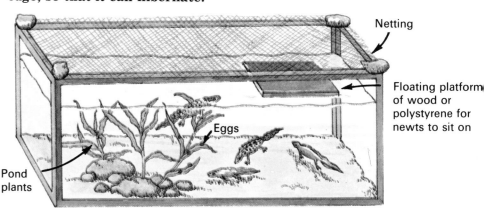

Plants

Sunken dish of drinking water

Half a flowerpot for the toad to hide in

Wooden box (25 cm high) filled with earth

How to collect: Visit ponds in the breeding season (March, April) at night. If you hear a male toad croaking, shine a torch at him. When the light hits his eyes, he will not move. Take the toad home in a wet plastic box with air holes.

Where to keep: Make a box like this. Put netting on top to keep the toad in. Put it in the shade, either in the garden or indoors. Handle it with wet hands. In the autumn, return it to the pond's edge, so that it can hibernate.

Feeding: Feed the toad twice a week with live earthworms, slugs and insects. Offer it small pieces of meat held in tweezers and moved about to look alive. Keep the dish filled with fresh water.

Newts

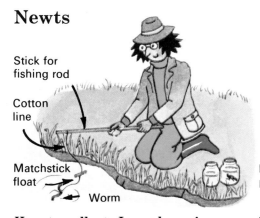

Stick for fishing rod

Cotton line

Matchstick float

Worm

Netting

Floating platform of wood or polystyrene for newts to sit on

Eggs

Pond plants

How to collect: In early spring, fish for newts or catch them in a net. When the newt bites the worm bait, pull the line in. Take it home in a jar with some pond water.

Where to keep: Keep newts in an aquarium in a light place. Take them back to the edge of the same pond in August, so that they can find a place to hibernate.

Feeding: If the newts mate and tadpoles hatch, feed them on Water Fleas from the pond. Feed adult newts on earthworms and small bits of raw meat dropped into the water.

Other Water Animals

Worms and Leeches

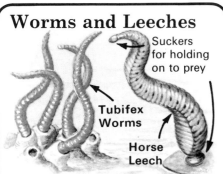

Suckers for holding on to prey

Tubifex Worms

Horse Leech

There are many kinds of worms and leeches in fresh water. The Tubifex Worm lives head down in a tube of mud. Leeches swim about hunting for fishes, frogs, larvae and snails.

Hydras

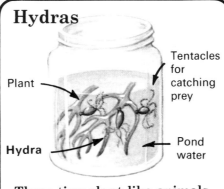

Plant

Tentacles for catching prey

Hydra

Pond water

These tiny plant-like animals contract into blobs if disturbed. Leave some water plants in water for an hour to see if there are any Hydras attached to them.

Bubble of air

Water Spider   Water Mites

Only one spider lives under water. It spins a web between plants, then fills it with air collected on its body from the surface. The spider can stay in this "diving bell" for a long time, without surfacing for air. Look, too, for the tiny Water Mites which are related to spiders.

Animals with Shells

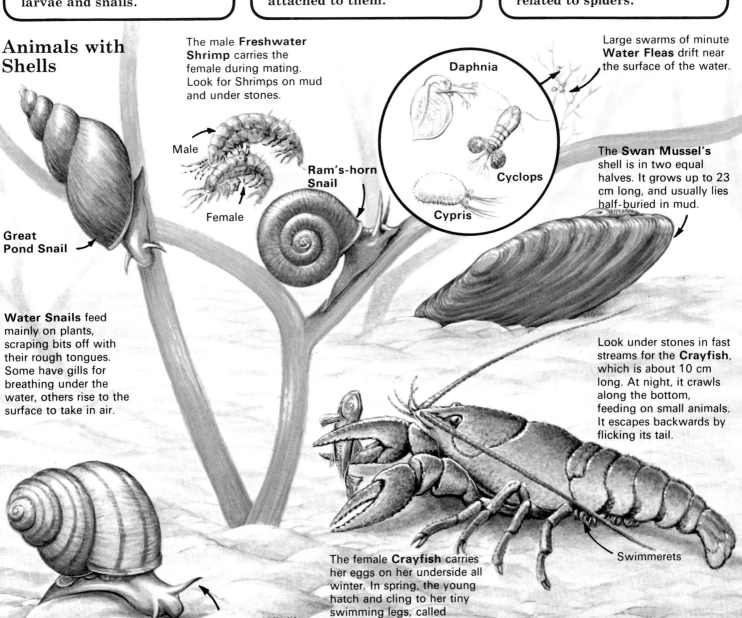

The male **Freshwater Shrimp** carries the female during mating. Look for Shrimps on mud and under stones.

Male

Female

Ram's-horn Snail

Daphnia

Cyclops

Cypris

Large swarms of minute **Water Fleas** drift near the surface of the water.

The **Swan Mussel's** shell is in two equal halves. It grows up to 23 cm long, and usually lies half-buried in mud.

Great Pond Snail

Water Snails feed mainly on plants, scraping bits off with their rough tongues. Some have gills for breathing under the water, others rise to the surface to take in air.

Look under stones in fast streams for the **Crayfish**, which is about 10 cm long. At night, it crawls along the bottom, feeding on small animals. It escapes backwards by flicking its tail.

Swimmerets

The female **Crayfish** carries her eggs on her underside all winter. In spring, the young hatch and cling to her tiny swimming legs, called swimmerets.

Freshwater Winkle

More Freshwater Life to Spot

Fishes

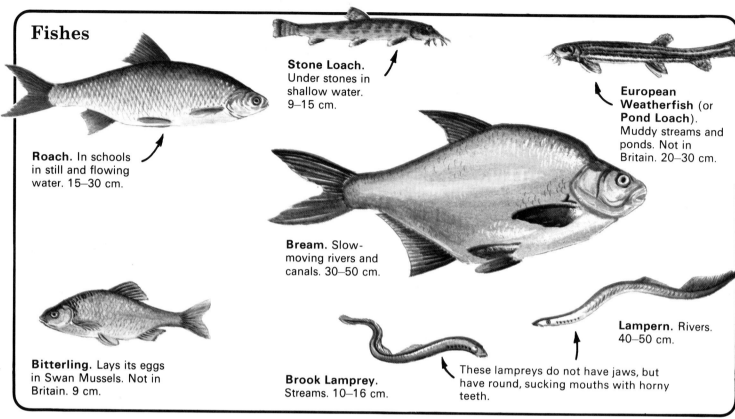

Roach. In schools in still and flowing water. 15–30 cm.

Stone Loach. Under stones in shallow water. 9–15 cm.

European Weatherfish (or **Pond Loach**). Muddy streams and ponds. Not in Britain. 20–30 cm.

Bream. Slow-moving rivers and canals. 30–50 cm.

Bitterling. Lays its eggs in Swan Mussels. Not in Britain. 9 cm.

Brook Lamprey. Streams. 10–16 cm.

Lampern. Rivers. 40–50 cm.

These lampreys do not have jaws, but have round, sucking mouths with horny teeth.

Plants

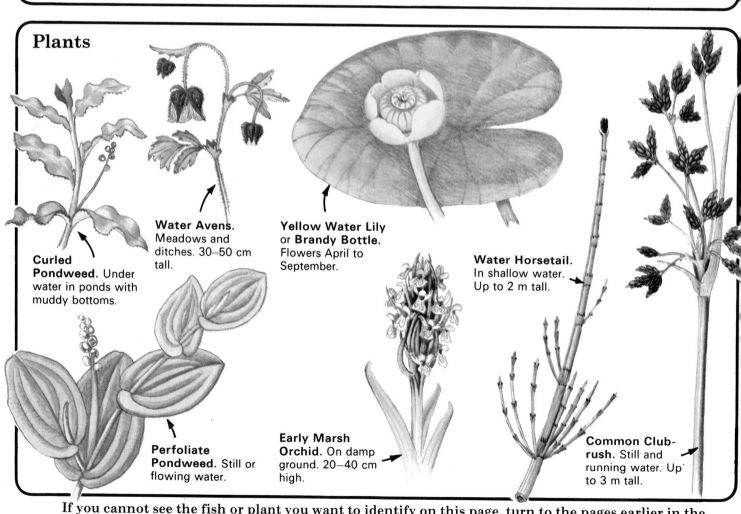

Curled Pondweed. Under water in ponds with muddy bottoms.

Water Avens. Meadows and ditches. 30–50 cm tall.

Yellow Water Lily or **Brandy Bottle.** Flowers April to September.

Water Horsetail. In shallow water. Up to 2 m tall.

Perfoliate Pondweed. Still or flowing water.

Early Marsh Orchid. On damp ground. 20–40 cm high.

Common Clubrush. Still and running water. Up to 3 m tall.

If you cannot see the fish or plant you want to identify on this page, turn to the pages earlier in the book that deal with these things.

Toads

Common Toad. Hides under stones or tree roots in day. Often in gardens. Female to 12 cm. Male 6 cm.

Natterjack Toad. Sandy and stony places. Digs holes to shelter in. Rare. 6–8 cm.

Green Toad. Green shade changes to match background. Not in Britain. 6–9 cm.

Yellow-bellied Toad

Underside

The **Fire-bellied Toad** and the **Yellow-bellied Toad** live in water. Show off bright warning colours when alarmed. Not in Britain. 4–5 cm.

Fire-bellied Toad

Spadefoot Toad. Burrows with spade-like growths on feet. Smells like garlic. Not in Britain. 6–8 cm.

Frogs

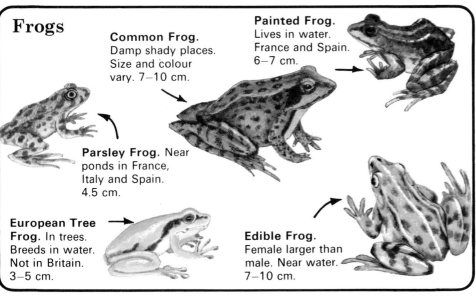

Common Frog. Damp shady places. Size and colour vary. 7–10 cm.

Painted Frog. Lives in water. France and Spain. 6–7 cm.

Parsley Frog. Near ponds in France, Italy and Spain. 4.5 cm.

European Tree Frog. In trees. Breeds in water. Not in Britain. 3–5 cm.

Edible Frog. Female larger than male. Near water. 7–10 cm.

Tortoise

European Pond Tortoise. Muddy ponds and marshes. Central and southern Europe. Up to 36 cm.

Newts

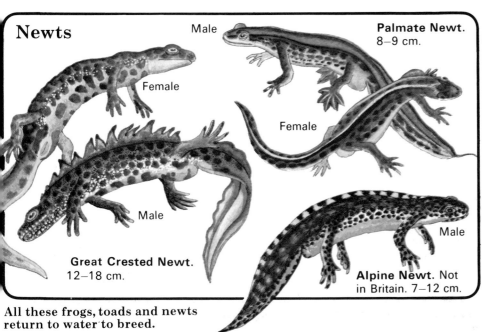

Male

Female

Palmate Newt. 8–9 cm.

Female

Male

Great Crested Newt. 12–18 cm.

Alpine Newt. Not in Britain. 7–12 cm.

All these frogs, toads and newts return to water to breed.

Snakes

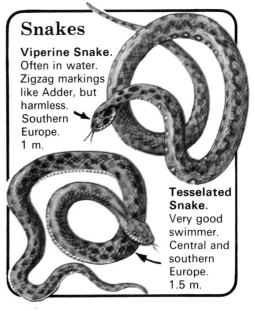

Viperine Snake. Often in water. Zigzag markings like Adder, but harmless. Southern Europe. 1 m.

Tesselated Snake. Very good swimmer. Central and southern Europe. 1.5 m.

Water Insects and their Young

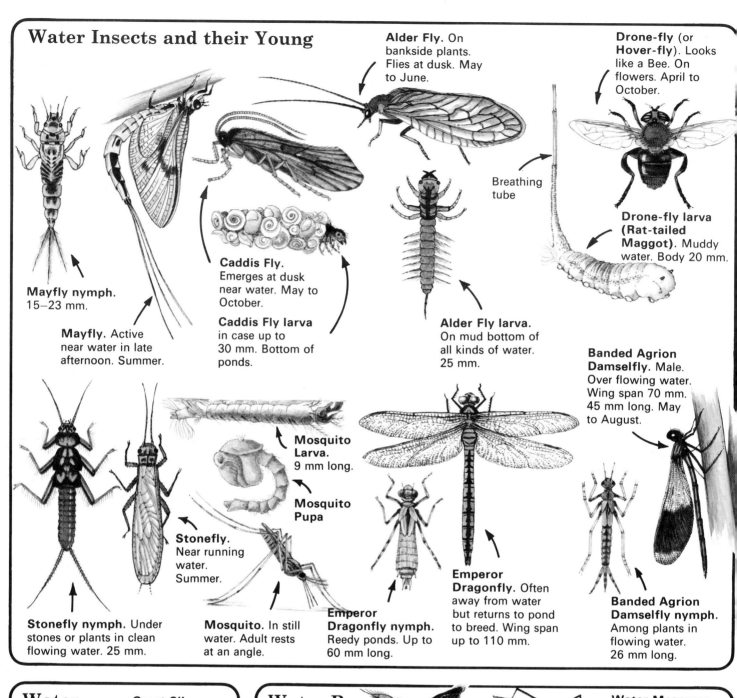

Mayfly nymph. 15–23 mm.

Mayfly. Active near water in late afternoon. Summer.

Caddis Fly. Emerges at dusk near water. May to October.

Caddis Fly larva in case up to 30 mm. Bottom of ponds.

Alder Fly. On bankside plants. Flies at dusk. May to June.

Breathing tube

Alder Fly larva. On mud bottom of all kinds of water. 25 mm.

Drone-fly (or Hover-fly). Looks like a Bee. On flowers. April to October.

Drone-fly larva (Rat-tailed Maggot). Muddy water. Body 20 mm.

Stonefly nymph. Under stones or plants in clean flowing water. 25 mm.

Stonefly. Near running water. Summer.

Mosquito Larva. 9 mm long.

Mosquito Pupa

Mosquito. In still water. Adult rests at an angle.

Emperor Dragonfly nymph. Reedy ponds. Up to 60 mm long.

Emperor Dragonfly. Often away from water but returns to pond to breed. Wing span up to 110 mm.

Banded Agrion Damselfly. Male. Over flowing water. Wing span 70 mm. 45 mm long. May to August.

Banded Agrion Damselfly nymph. Among plants in flowing water. 26 mm long.

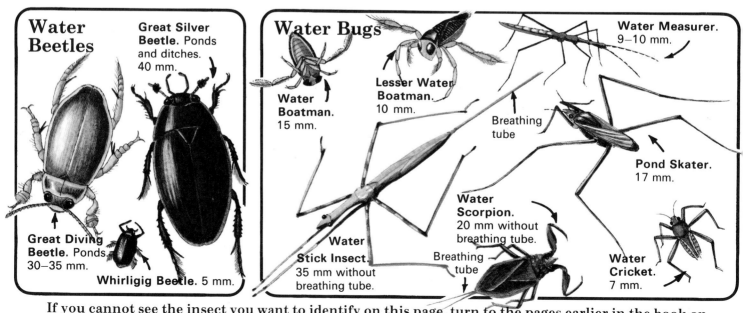

Water Beetles

Great Silver Beetle. Ponds and ditches. 40 mm.

Great Diving Beetle. Ponds. 30–35 mm.

Whirligig Beetle. 5 mm.

Water Bugs

Water Boatman. 15 mm.

Lesser Water Boatman. 10 mm.

Breathing tube

Water Measurer. 9–10 mm.

Pond Skater. 17 mm.

Water Stick Insect. 35 mm without breathing tube.

Water Scorpion. 20 mm without breathing tube.

Breathing tube

Water Cricket. 7 mm.

If you cannot see the insect you want to identify on this page, turn to the pages earlier in the book on insects, where you may be able to see a picture of it.

Birds

Measurements are from beak to tip of tail.

Grey Heron. Nests in trees. Feeds in shallow water and marshes. 90 cm.

Osprey. Dives to catch fish in claws. Rare. A few breed in Scotland. 51–58 cm.

Mallard. Most common duck. Often in parks. 58 cm.

Male

Female

Chick

Great Crested Grebe. In lakes and reservoirs. Winters also on coast. 48 cm.

Winter

Summer

Female

Male

Teal. Europe's smallest duck. 35 cm.

Coot. Lives in flocks outside breeding season. Notice white mark on head. 38 cm.

Chick

Snipe. Hides among plants near water, where it feeds. Long bill for probing in mud. 27 cm.

Chick

Moorhen. Common in parks. Notice white flash under tail. 33 cm.

Water Rail. Hides in reed beds. 28 cm.

Summer

Winter

Black-headed Gull. Loses dark cap in winter. 35–38 cm.

Spotted Crake. White spotted body. Feeds at water edge at dusk. Very secretive. 23 cm.

Swallow. Summer visitor. Catches insects on the wing. 19 cm.

Yellow Wagtail. Lives in Britain. **Blue-headed Wagtail** in Central Europe. Other varieties in Europe (see below). 16.5 cm.

Yellow Wagtail

Pied Wagtail

Female

Blue-headed Wagtail

Male

Scandinavia

White Wagtail. Lives in Europe. **Pied Wagtail** in Britain. 18 cm.

White Wagtail

Grey Wagtail. Lives near fast-flowing streams. 18 cm.

Italy

Spain and France

Reed Bunting. By rivers and in marshy places. 15 cm.

If you cannot see the bird you want to identify on this page, turn to the pages earlier in the book on birds, and you may be able to see a picture of it.

Index